Introducing Seattle

Though it's long been known for its gray skies and strong coffee, Seattle's reputation is staked on the stunning natural beauty of the surrounding area, a vibrant arts community and a population that's as well read as any in the United States.

With a temperate maritime climate and a wealth of outdoor activities within an hour's drive, Seattle has long been a haven for outdoor enthusiasts. But the Emerald City has evolved into something much greater than just an evergreen-streaked metropolis sandwiched between Lake Washington and Puget Sound.

The region's technology industry, led by corporate giants like Microsoft and Amazon.com, has sent housing prices rocketing into the stratosphere, and the city's Downtown is experiencing an unparalleled condominium construction boom and waterfront regeneration. Thriving programs at the University of Washington and the Fred Hutchinson Cancer Research Center have helped transform Seattle into the nation's fifth-largest center for biomedical research and development.

The city's famed music scene, which rose to international prominence thanks to forefathers like Jimi Hendrix, Nirvana and Pearl Jam, is still going strong. New gourmet pubs, bistros and fine-dining restaurants appear every year, along with some of the nation's finest chefs, and foodies flock to join the creative culinary tours (▷ 123). This cultural renaissance is the result of continued gentrification; neighborhoods such as Central District, which once were the domain of low-income residents, are now populated by youthful, moneyed technology workers.

Seattle's geographic location has ensured its continued success as a portal for trade along the Pacific Rim. Aside from the city's lack of an effective mass-transit system, Seattle is one of the country's most powerful and vital civic hubs.

Facts + Figures

- **Estimated visitors in 2013: 18.6 million**
- **Approximate amount of dollars spent by visitors in 2013: $6 billion**
- **Number of Downtown hotel rooms available: 12,750**

MOUNTAINS UPON MOUNTAINS

Seattle sits between two soaring mountain ranges. The Cascade Mountains lie to the east of the city—dominated by snow-capped Mt. Baker—while the sawlike ridges of the Olympic Range frame the western sky. Both ranges can be seen from many neighborhoods in the city, but the best views can be found on Queen Anne Hill.

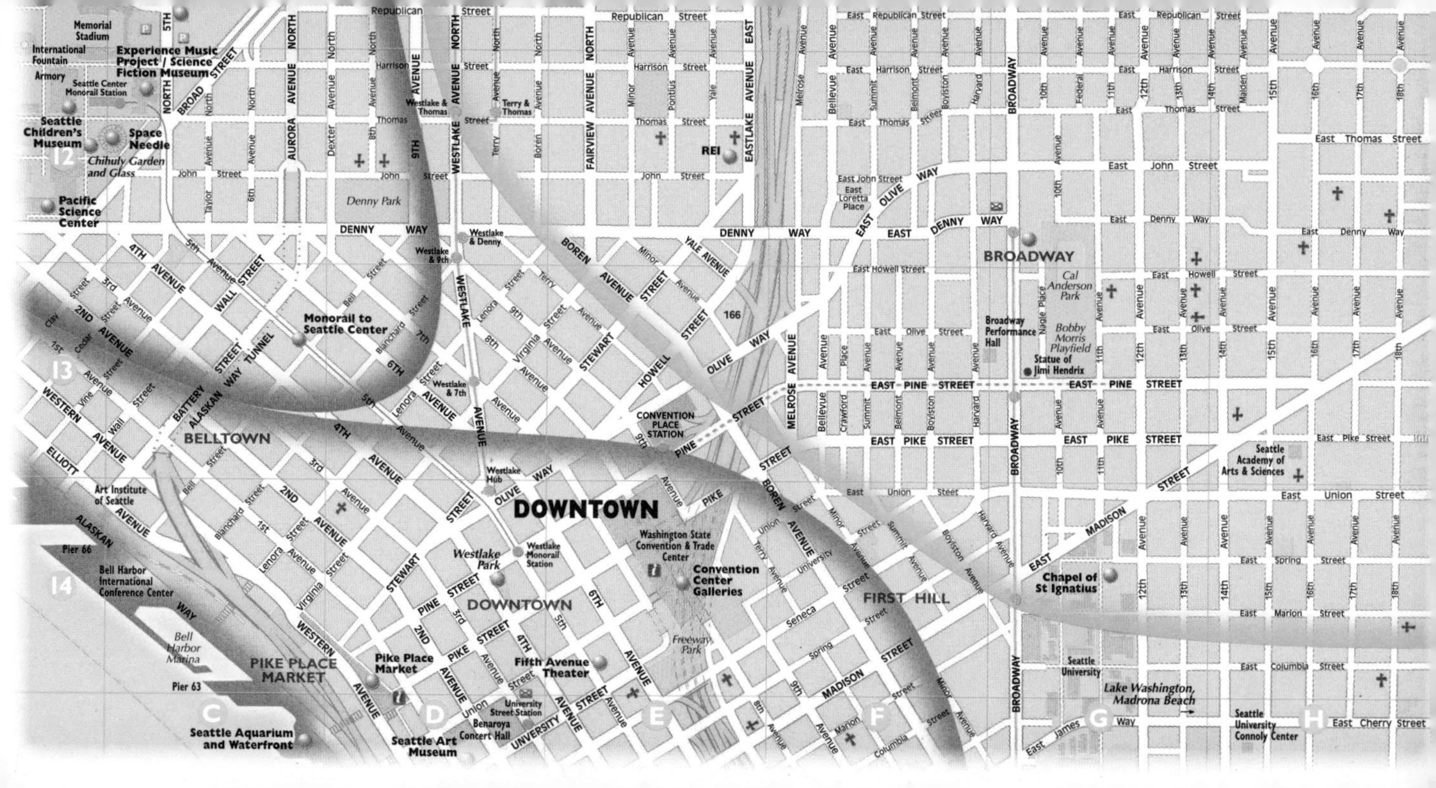

DOWNTOWN
BELLTOWN
BROADWAY
FIRST HILL
PIKE PLACE MARKET
Memorial Stadium
International Fountain
Armory
Seattle Center Monorail Station
Experience Music Project / Science Fiction Museum
Seattle Children's Museum
Space Needle
Chihuly Garden and Glass
Pacific Science Center
Denny Park
REI
Monorail to Seattle Center
Westlake & Thomas
Terry & Thomas
Westlake & Denny
Westlake & 9th
Westlake & 7th
Westlake Hub
Westlake Monorail Station
Westlake Park
Convention Place Station
Washington State Convention & Trade Center
Convention Center Galleries
Freeway Park
Fifth Avenue Theater
University Street Station
Benaroya Concert Hall
Seattle Art Museum
Pike Place Market
Seattle Aquarium and Waterfront
Pier 63
Pier 66
Bell Harbor Marina
Bell Harbor International Conference Center
Art Institute of Seattle
Broadway Performance Hall
Cal Anderson Park
Bobby Morris Playfield
Statue of Jimi Hendrix
Seattle Academy of Arts & Sciences
Chapel of St Ignatius
Seattle University
Seattle University Connoly Center
Lake Washington, Madrona Beach
DENNY WAY
EAST PINE STREET
EAST PIKE STREET
MADISON STREET
BROADWAY
WESTLAKE AVENUE
ALASKAN WAY
WESTERN AVENUE
ELLIOTT AVENUE
BATTERY STREET TUNNEL
12
13
14
C
D
E
F
G
H
166

Fodor's

25 Best

SEATTLE

How to Use This Book

KEY TO SYMBOLS

- Map reference to the accompanying fold-out map
- Address
- Telephone number
- Opening/closing times
- Restaurant or café
- Nearest rail station
- Nearest bus route
- Nearest riverboat or ferry stop
- Facilities for visitors with disabilities
- Other practical information
- Further information
- Tourist information
- Admission charges: Expensive (more than $17) Moderate ($10–$17) Inexpensive ($9 or less)

This guide is divided into four sections

• Essential Seattle: An introduction to the city and tips on making the most of your stay.
• Seattle by Area: We've broken the city into six areas, and recommended the best sights, shops, entertainment venues, nightlife and restaurants in each one. Suggested walks help you to explore on foot.
• Where to Stay: The best hotels, whether you're looking for luxury, budget or something in between.
• Need to Know: The info you need to make your trip run smoothly, including getting about by public transportation, weather tips, emergency phone numbers and useful websites.

Navigation In the Seattle by Area chapter, we've given each area its own color, which is also used on the locator maps throughout the book and the map on the inside front cover.

Maps The fold-out map accompanying this book is a comprehensive street plan of Seattle. The grid on this fold-out map is the same as the grid on the locator maps within the book. We've given grid references within the book for each sight and listing.

CITY OF WATER

Seattle is between two significant bodies of water. To the west is Puget Sound, a sprawling arm of the Pacific Ocean that reaches all the way from Whidbey Island, 30 miles (48km) north of Seattle, to Olympia, 50 miles (80km) south of Seattle. To the east is Lake Washington, one of the country's largest urban lakes.

BIRTHPLACE OF THE BEAN

In 1971, three local entrepreneurs opened a small coffeehouse just below the Pike Place Market. They named their shop after a caffeine-crazed first mate in Melville's *Moby Dick*: Starbucks. Their venture has since become the largest coffeehouse company in the world, with more than 17,000 locations across the globe.

A Short Stay in Seattle

DAY 1

Morning Take a taxi to Queen Anne Hill, a historic (and gorgeous) neighborhood north of Downtown. The hill is one of the city's tallest—its summit is 456ft (139m) above Puget Sound. Stop in for a hearty breakfast at the **5 Spot** café (⊳ 56), hit the shops on Queen Anne Avenue, and don't miss the stellar Downtown views from **Kerry Park Viewpoint** (⊳ 54).

Mid-morning Walk along the waterfront, basking in the cool sea breeze that wafts off Elliott Bay. Stop in at the **Seattle Aquarium** (⊳ 30–31), with exhibits featuring shorebirds, six-gill sharks, tide pools and cute sea otters.

Lunch Hop on the **Bainbridge Island Ferry** (⊳ 25) to Winslow, a can't-miss 35-minute ride across Puget Sound. Stroll Winslow's quaint boulevards and lunch on great fish-and-chips at the Harbor Public House.

Afternoon Upon returning to Seattle's Colman dock, walk eastward up the **Harbor Steps** (⊳ 34) into **Downtown** Seattle (⊳ 32–33) proper. Visit the stunning **Seattle Art Museum** (⊳ 32–33) before heading toward the "retail core", the four-block goldmine of high-end shops and department stores that surround Pine Street, between 5th and 7th avenues.

Dinner Cash in on your early planning by being on time for your reservation at **Loulay** (⊳ 43), where chef Thiery Rautureau adds his magic to a menu driven by the finest local ingredients—without breaking the bank. Start with smoked salmon with fava beans, followed by a succulent rib-eye with confit shallot and red wine demi-glace.

Evening Walk south along 1st Avenue toward **Pioneer Square** (⊳ 27) and its mind-boggling array of bars and lounges, many of which feature live music nightly.

DAY 2

Morning Ride Seattle's **Monorail** (⊳ 50) then use the city bus system—which is renowned for its ecoconscious hybrid and electrically powered vehicles—to get to the leafy neighborhood of Madrona, east of Downtown. Have breakfast at another popular spot: the Hi Spot Café, home to some of the city's best fresh-baked scones.

Mid-morning Explore the **Washington Park Arboretum** (⊳ 65), a 230-acre (93ha) oasis of botanical diversity in Seattle's Montlake neighborhood. The Arboretum, which is maintained by the nearby **University of Washington** (⊳ 77), has North America's largest collection of maple and sorbus trees, along with a renowned Japanese Garden.

Lunch If the weather cooperates, enjoy an outdoor lunch at **Agua Verde** (⊳ 82), a standout Mexican-inspired eatery on the shores of Portage Bay.

Afternoon Walk north from Agua Verde along **University Way** (⊳ 77), the cultural and culinary hub of the University of Washington. Shop for music at one of the many record stores before visiting the university's **Henry Art Gallery** (⊳ 76). Travel to **Capitol Hill** (⊳ 60–61), the bustling nexus of Seattle's artistic community. This area is loaded with funky boutiques, preeminent bistros and nightclubs. Stroll along **Broadway** (⊳ 60), which provides the heartbeat of the city's cultural life.

Dinner Stop in at one of Capitol Hill's incredible bistros—**Lark** and **Café Presse** (⊳ 70) rank among the best.

Evening Head down the hill into Downtown and catch a show at Benaroya Hall, home to the Seattle Symphony. Or head north to Seattle Center for a performance by the **Seattle Opera** (⊳ 56) in McCaw Hall.

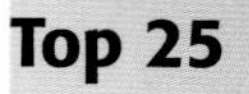

Top 25

Alki Beach and West Seattle ▷ 100–101 Sandy beaches, incredible views and a lively street scene.

Burke Museum of Natural History and Culture ▷ 74–75 Objects from across Washington State.

Capitol Hill ▷ 60–61 The cultural hub—a must-see if you want to sample bohemian Seattle.

Chihuly Garden and Glass ▷ 48 Stunning modern glass art set in a garden and gallery.

Chinatown-International District ▷ 24 A local treasure featuring restaurants serving Asian cuisine.

Discovery Park ▷ 86–87 The city's largest park sits on Magnolia Bluff, with incredible views of Puget Sound.

Experience Music Project/Science Fiction Museum ▷ 49 A madcap rock 'n' roll and sci-fi museum.

Ferry to Bainbridge Island ▷ 25 The world's third-largest ferry system offers a breathtaking ride.

Future of Flight Aviation Center and Boeing Tour ▷ 102 Tour the Boeing aircraft factory and design your own airplane.

Henry Art Gallery ▷ 76 The UW's own art museum shows contemporary American masters.

Hiram M. Chittenden Locks ▷ 88–89 Ballard's main attraction connects Washington to Puget Sound.

Lake Union ▷ 62–63 The city's best spot for kayaking, sailboat-watching and on-the-water relaxation.

Monorail to Seattle Center ▷ 50 The nation's first commercial monorail runs along an elevated track.

Museum of Flight ▷ 103 A collection of fighter aircraft and a treasure trove of historical aviation.

Olympic Sculpture Park ▷ 26 Monumental works of art in a lovely waterfront park.

Pacific Science Center ▷ 51 Hands-on science museum, complete with an enormous IMAX theater.

Pike Place Market ▷ 28–29 A local icon in a Downtown location overlooking Elliott Bay.

Pioneer Square ▷ 27 Seattle's oldest neighborhood is now a center of the city's nightlife scene.

REI ▷ 64 The outdoor equipment mega-retailer's flagship store is a destination unto itself.

Seattle Aquarium and the Waterfront ▷ 30–31 Authentic piers, curiosity shops and aquarium along a waterfront promenade.

Seattle Art Museum ▷ 32–33 Expanded in 2008 and more beautiful than ever, featuring 70,000sq ft (6,500sq m) of gallery space.

Space Needle ▷ 52–53 The city's signature landmark towers above Seattle Center.

University of Washington ▷ 77 UW's campus is one of Seattle's most breathtaking attributes.

Washington Park Arboretum ▷ 65 An urban oasis of woody plants, elegant gardens and winding forest pathways.

Woodland Park Zoo ▷ 90–91 One of the nation's finest zoos, with more than 300 species.

These pages are a quick guide to the Top 25, which are described in more detail later. Here they are listed alphabetically, and the tinted background shows which area they are in.

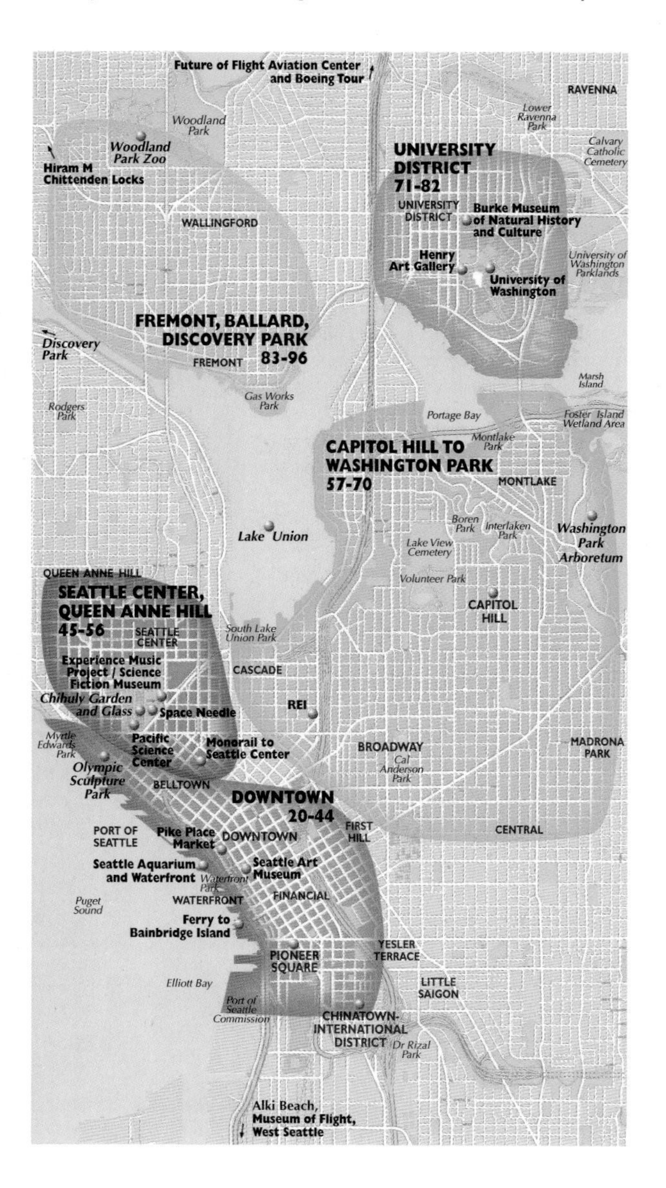

Shopping

Markets play a big part in Seattle life (center); while Westlake Center(above) offers a mall experience

Greater Downtown has been a shopping destination since the Alaska Gold Rush, when the city became the chief outfitting post for prospectors heading north. One lucky miner returned with a small nest egg to start a retail shoe business that has since grown into Seattle's most cherished department store—Nordstrom (▷ 39), renowned for its customer service.

Pike Place Market

For small gifts, start at Pike Place Market, where farmers and artisans set up their stalls before 9am. The tables displaying fresh flower bouquets often carry dried arrangements that make excellent gifts. In the crafts area you'll find wood and metal items, as well as pottery, jewelry, textiles and regional food items like preserves, dried cherries and smoked fish.

Sample the Wares

Washington wines, having garnered top awards at international tastings, are another special purchase. Grapes are grown east of Washington's Cascade Range at the same latitude as the wine-making provinces of France—Pike Market Cellars offers a good selection. You can sample the local wines at one of the tasting rooms close to the city—try Chateau Ste. Michelle (▷ 104), 15 miles northeast of Downtown in Woodinville, Washington state's oldest winery (founded in 1934). To re-create Northwest cuisine at home, stop at Post Alley for a look at local cookbooks penned by world-class Seattle chefs like Tom Douglas. Cookbooks are also

SEATTLE'S SALES TAX

Don't be surprised at the 9.5 percent sales tax added to your purchases. Many locals believe this tax places an unfair burden on poor people and favor, instead, a state income tax (Washington has none). In this economic climate, however, it's unlikely that voters would approve a totally new levy. For better or worse, the sales tax is probably here to stay.

Ye Olde Curiosity Shop on Fisherman's Wharf (top); browsing the shopping streets of Belltown (above)

available at the Made in Washington (⊳ 39) shop, which carries only items that are made, produced or grown in the state. Seattle is well-known for its glass art, primarily through the work of Dale Chihuly and other glass-blowers working in the tradition of the Pilchuck Glass School in Stanford (50 miles/81km north of Seattle), who exhibit and sell their brilliant wares in galleries and studios throughout the city. For the tacky and the bizarre, check out the tourist haunts along Seattle's waterfront and the funky shops in Fremont. For joke and novelty items, you can't beat Archie McPhee & Co. (1300 N 45th Street) in the Wallingford neighborhood.

Dedicated Shoppers

Today, to find the greatest variety of stores in a compact area head straight for the Downtown retail core, the Pike Place Market and neighboring Belltown and Pioneer Square. Seattle reigns as a manufacturer and retailer of outdoor and recreational apparel. There are outfitters both Downtown and in the South Lake Union neighborhood, where REI (⊳ 64) resides. Visit Downtown department stores and upscale malls like Westlake Center and Pacific Place—or check out Belltown designer boutiques along 1st and 2nd avenues from Bell Steet.

FINE ART

Seattle's fine arts galleries and craft shops are concentrated in Downtown malls, around the Seattle Art Museum and in Pioneer Square. Many feature Native American art of the Northwest Coast. You will find not only antiques—Native American baskets, jewelry, early Edward Curtis photographs, ceremonial masks and wood carvings—but also striking contemporary prints and carvings created by Native American artists working today. Fine woodworking is also on display at the cooperative Northwest Woodworkers Gallery (⊳ 39), a furniture showroom. Here you can view exceptional craftsmanship and one-of-a-kind designs, and commission a piece by the artist of your choice.

Shopping by Theme

From specialty shops to large-scale department stores, Seattle's shopping culture is booming. On this page, shops are listed by theme. For a more detailed write-up, see the individual listings in Seattle by Area.

ART/ANTIQUES

ArtFX (▷ 95)
Azuma Gallery (▷ 37)
Flanagan & Lane Antiques (▷ 38)
Flury & Co. Gallery (▷ 38)
Fremont Vintage Mall (▷ 95)
Ghost Gallery (▷ 69)
Glasshouse Studio (▷ 38)
Greg Kucera Gallery (▷ 38)
Isadora's (▷ 38)
Kirsten Gallery (▷ 80)
The Legacy (▷ 39)
Northwest Woodworkers Gallery (▷ 39)
Traver Gallery(▷ 39)

BOOKS/MUSIC

Bulldog News (▷ 80)
Elliott Bay Book Company (▷ 69)
Seattle Mystery Bookshop (▷ 39)
Sonic Boom Records (▷ 69)
Twice-Sold Tales (▷ 69)
University Bookstore (▷ 80)

CLOTHES/ ACCESSORIES

Alhambra (▷ 37)
Les Amis (▷ 95)
Ann Taylor (▷ 37)
Anthropologie (▷ 37)
Baby & Co. (▷ 37)
Banana Republic (▷ 37)
Barneys (▷ 37)
BCBG (▷ 37)
Brooks Brothers (▷ 37)
Bryn Walker (▷ 80)
Butch Blum (▷ 37)
Chicos (▷ 37)
Earth, Wind & Fire (▷ 37)
Eddie Bauer (▷ 38)
Edie's Shoes (▷ 69)
Eileen Fisher (▷ 38)
Endless Knot (▷ 38)
Filson (▷ 38)
Hub & Bespoke (▷ 95)
J. Crew (▷ 38)
Kuhlman (▷ 38)
Mario's (▷ 39)
Moksha Clothing & Accessories (▷ 80)
Nordstrom (▷ 39)
Patagonia (▷ 39)
Re-soul (▷ 95)
Show Pony Boutique (▷ 95)
Sway & Cake (▷ 39)
Thistle Accessoire (▷ 95)
Urban Outfitters (▷ 69)
Wooly Mammoth (▷ 80)

GIFTS

Caldwell's (▷ 80)
Made in Washington (▷ 39)
Phoenix Rising Gallery (▷ 39)
Portage Bay Goods (▷ 95)

KITSCH, FUNK, RETRO

Buffalo Exchange (▷ 80)
Gold Dogs Vintage (▷ 95)
Le Frock (▷ 69)

MALLS/MARKETS

Farmer's Market (▷ panel, 96)
University Village (▷ 80)

SPECIALTY SHOPS

Agate Designs (▷ 37)
Artist and Craftsman Supply (▷ 80)
Bella Umbrella (▷ 37)
Facere Jewelry Art (▷ 38)
Fox's Gem Shop (▷ 38)
Magic Mouse (▷ 39)
Market Magic Shop (▷ 39)
Theo Chocolate (▷ 95)
Vegan Haven ▷ 80)
World Spice Merchants (▷ 39)
Woven Art (▷ 39)

Seattle by Night

As the sun sets off Whidbey Island (middle), the city is illuminated, and the Space Needle steals the show (top); Glasshouse, Chihuly Garden and Glass (bottom)

After-hours entertainment in Seattle runs the gamut from classical music to spectator sports, comedy to swing dance.

Performance Arts

The Seattle Opera, Pacific Northwest Ballet, Seattle Symphony, and several theater companies are in residence between late fall and early summer In May and June, the city hosts the Seattle International Film Festival. At any given time during the rest of the year, a half-dozen local cinemas are showing foreign or independent films. Concert venues like the Paramount (⊳ 41) and Fifth Avenue (⊳ 40) book touring artists all the time, and local theater companies stagger their plays so that audiences can enjoy live theater in every month.

Summer Nightlife

In summer, an evening of baseball is fun; when Mariners' action flags, take a minute to check out the view from Safeco Field's upper deck (⊳ 41). Another pleasant option is a twilight ferry ride across Elliott Bay. Summer days are long—perfect for an evening stroll while it's still light, followed by drinks and dinner on the patio of a waterfront restaurant.

Cooler Months

On a cold winter's evening, stop for a cocktail at a swanky hotel lounge, quench your thirst at a Belltown tavern, or see what's on tap at one of Seattle's excellent brewpubs. Seattle's many clubs (⊳ panel) host live music, dancing, comedy or improvisational theater.

CLUBS FOR ALL

Belltown hangouts that once played grunge now feature hip-hop, while other Downtown nightclubs cater to an older, more upscale crowd that enjoys salsa dancing or listening to jazz. Pioneer Square has both stylish clubs and taverns that draw young singles. For acoustic music, head to Ballard, where the atmosphere is more laid-back. Capitol Hill along Pike and Pine is home to the city's gay bars and clubs.

Eating Out

Seattle's continued economic and cultural growth has spurred a culinary renaissance, and the city has experienced a boom in top-flight restaurants. Along with them came an armada of diners with educated palates and ample wallets. The result: brilliant restaurants that push the borders of traditional Pacific Northwestern cuisine.

Restaurants abound in Downtown Seattle: from all-weather Pacific Place (top) to a quiet al fresco corner of Pioneer Square (bottom)

Pick and Choose

Thanks to its large geographical footprint—and its group of adorable outlying neighborhoods—prospective diners often plan their evenings around their choice of restaurant. For instance: Diners heading to a special-occasion meal at the Canlis (▷ 96) often catch an après-dinner band in Ballard's historical district before heading home.

Seafood Central

With the city's proximity to fresh seafood, it makes sense that Seattle's seafood restaurants rank among the best in the country. In the summer months, wild Alaskan salmon is the headliner; wintertime favorites include Alaskan halibut and king crab. Plus, the local oysters and mussels are not to be missed.

When to Go

Breakfast is sometimes served all day at coffee shops and diners, but typical breakfast hours are from 7 to 11am. Lunch begins at 11am and concludes by 3pm; whereas dinner begins at 5pm and finishes at 9pm during the week and 10 or 11pm on weekends. Brunch is becoming increasingly popular in Seattle.

TAXES AND TIPPING

The city of Seattle adds a sales tax of 9.5 percent to restaurant bills; on top of that, customers are expected to add at least 15 percent gratuity. (That's assuming the meal was satisfactory, of course.) For the vast majority of diners, a 20 percent tip is standard—especially at the city's upscale eateries.

Restaurants by Cuisine

The following restaurants are intended to suit all tastes and budgets in Seattle. On this page, they are listed by cuisine. For a more detailed descripton of each restaurant, see Seattle by Area.

ASIAN/SUSHI

Araya's Place (▷ 70)
Dragonfish Asian Café (▷ 42)
Malay Satay Hut (▷ panel, 43)
Maneki (▷ 43)
Ohana (▷ 43)
Tamarind Tree (▷ 44)
Wild Ginger (▷ 44)

COFFEE/PASTRY

Bauhaus (▷ 42)
Café Besalu (▷ 96)
Caffè Ladro (▷ 70)
Espresso Vivace (▷ 70)
Herkimer Coffee (▷ 96)
Macrina Bakery (▷ 43)
Panama Hotel Tea & Coffee House (▷ 43)
Queen Bee Café (▷ 70)
Seattle Bagel Bakery (▷ panel, 44)
Zeitgeist Kunst and Kaffee (▷ 44)

EUROPEAN

Altura (▷ 70)
Aragona (▷ 42)
Café Lago (▷ 82)
Die Bierstube (▷ 82)
Loulay (▷ 43)
Machiavelli (▷ 43)
Mad Pizza (▷ 96)
Pagliacci Pizza (▷ 82)
Pink Door (▷ 44)
Restaurant Marron (▷ 70)
Serafina (▷ 70)
Serious Pie (▷ 44)
Staple & Fancy (▷ 96)

MEXICAN/LATINO

Agua Verde (▷ 82)
El Camino (▷ 96)
Malena's Taco Shop (▷ 56)
Mama's Mexican Kitchen (▷ 43)
Tango Tapas Restaurant & Lounge (▷ 70)
Taqueria Guaymas (▷ 70)

NORTHWEST/ AMERICAN

5 Spot (▷ 56)
Canlis (▷ 96)
Dahlia Lounge (▷ 42)
Farestart (▷ panel, 42)
Frolik (▷ 42)
Hattie's Hat (▷ 96)
Jak's Grill (▷ 82)
The Metropolitan Grill (▷ 43)
Palace Kitchen (▷ 43)
Pine Box (▷ 70)
Portage Bay Café (▷ 82)
Salumi (▷ 44)
Shultzy's Sausage (▷ 82)
Skycity at the Needle (▷ 44)
Tilth (▷ 82)
Trace (▷ 44)

ROMANTIC BISTROS

Café Campagne (▷ 42)
Café Presse (▷ 70)
Crow (▷ 56)
Lark (▷ 70)
Matt's in the Market (▷ 43)
Pair (▷ 82)
Le Pichet (▷ 44)
Stumbling Goat Bistro (▷ 96)

SEAFOOD

Anthony's Homeport (▷ 96)
Ballard Annex Oyster House (▷ 96)
Brooklyn Seafood, Steak & Oyster Bar (▷ 42)
The Crab Pot (▷ 42)
Cutters (▷ 42)
Etta's Seafood (▷ 42)
Flying Fish (▷ 42)
Ivar's (▷ 43)
Jack's Fish Spot (▷ 43)
Pike Place Chowder (▷ 44)
Ray's Boathouse (▷ 96)
Restaurant Zoe (▷ 44)
Taylor Shellfish Farms Oyster Bar (▷ 44)

VEGETARIAN

Araya's Place (▷ 70)
Flowers (▷ 82)

Top Tips For...

However you'd like to spend your time in Seattle, these top suggestions should help you tailor your ideal visit. Each sight or listing has a larger write-up in Seattle by Area.

BUNKING IN BOUTIQUE HOTELS

Stop in for an early-evening cocktail at the Sorrento Hotel's (▷ 112) bar, the Fireside Room.
Relax with a glass of Washington wine at the Hotel Vintage (▷ 111), where each luxurious room is dedicated to a local vineyard or winery.
Enjoy a floor-to-ceiling view of Puget Sound and the Olympic Mountains from a room at the quaint Inn at the Market (▷ 112).

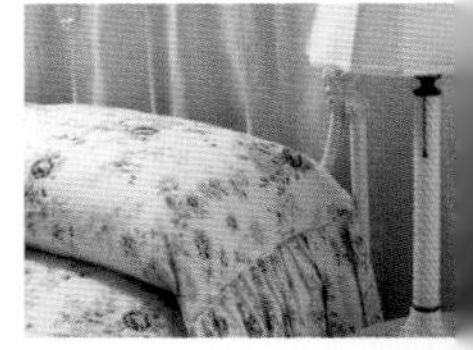

Comfy and stylish boutique hotels promise a good night's rest (top); the Center of the Universe sign in Fremont (above)

STROLLING SEATTLE'S NEIGHBORHOODS

Watch the salmon climb the fish ladder at Ballard's Hiram M. Chittenden Locks (▷ 88–89).
Explore the "Center of the Universe," also known as Fremont (▷ 92), Seattle's quirkiest area.
Walk down Azalea Way, a verdant greenway that snakes through Washington Park Arboretum (▷ 65).

THEATER AND FILM

Catch an independent or foreign film at the brick-walled historic art house, Harvard Exit (▷ 69).
Admire the Seattle Opera at McCaw Hall (▷ 56), a Seattle landmark venue.
Catch a Broadway musical at the ornate Fifth Avenue Theater (▷ 34).

DOING WHAT'S FREE

Amble through modern art at the Olympic Sculpture Park (▷ 26).
Gaze at the Stars at the University of Washington Observatory (▷ 81).
Catch the chamber music at the Frye Art Museum (▷ 34) on Sundays. afternoon

The opulent interior of the Fifth Avenue Theater (above right); Frye Art Museum (right)

hop 'til you drop, then ample the ocal ulinary elights

TOPPING UP THE WARDROBE

Try out the latest women's fashions at Les Amis in Ballard (▷ 95).

Designer menswear and impeccable service can be found at Kuhlman (▷ 38).

Stock up at Patagonia (▷ 39), with its unparalleled collection of outdoor clothing.

SAMPLING THE BEST BISTROS

Sample small-plate heaven at Lark (▷ 70), which has made its name on small plates and gourmet cocktails.

Bask in the warm glow of Altura (▷ 70), which specializes in Italian cuisine.

Escape to Paris in Café Campagne (▷ 42), a masterful combination of romantic atmosphere and gourmet French cuisine.

Hotel Max (above); Pacific Science Center (below)

LIVING THE HIGH LIFE

Dine at Canlis (▷ 96), the city's undisputed champion of high cuisine. The views, the food and the service are exemplary.

Stay at Hotel Max (▷ 111), one of the city's finest luxury hotels.

Get a bird's-eye view of the city and its fabulous coastal setting with a scenic flight by seaplane from Lake Union (▷ 62).

BRINGING THE KIDS

Science is hands-on at the Pacific Science Center (▷ 51), a family favorite.

Go to the top of the Space Needle (▷ 52–53). This legendary structure retains every bit of its space-age appeal.

Take them shopping at one of the city's specialty shops, such as the Market Magic Shop (▷ 39).

Joining friends for a drink (below)

EXPLORING ESPRESSO AND TEA

Grab a steaming cappuccino at the legendary coffeehouse, Bauhaus (▷ 42).
Buy yourself some beans at Herkimer Coffee (▷ 96), which sells fantastic java.
Soak up the vibe while you sip at the sidewalk café, Espresso Vivace (▷ 70).

DANCING INTO THE NIGHT

Go where the dancers are: Pioneer Square (▷ 27), packed with bars, dance clubs and pool halls.
Whoop it up in Belltown (▷ 13) at any one of the swanky clubs and cocktail lounges.
Get down with the hipsters on Capitol Hill (▷ 60–61), Seattle's most liberal neighborhood.

SHOPPING FOR SHOES

See the latest styles at Re-soul (▷ 95), which specializes in hard-to-find brands.
Don't miss Nordstrom (▷ 39) and its famous selection of men's and women's shoes.
Try on the stylish footwear at Wooly Mammoth (▷ 80) on University Way, where you will find brands including Chaco, Dankso and Clarks.

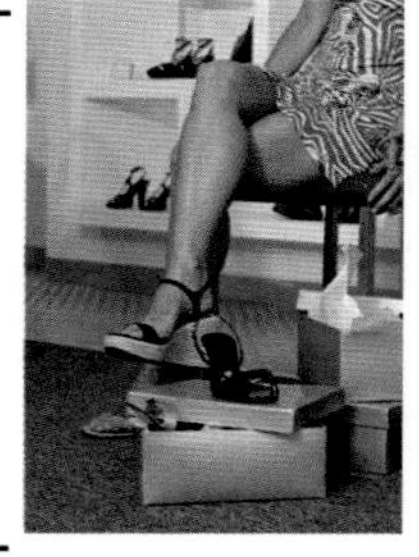

Treat yourself to new shoes before taking to the dance floor (above); take in a game (below)

THE SPORTING LIFE

Try to catch a baseball game during the summertime at Safeco Field (▷ 41), home of the Major League Mariners.
Rent a bright green bike for the day (▷ panel, 81) and explore the network of cycle routes and multi-use trails around the city.
Shop for outdoor gear at REI (▷ 64), the largest outdoor equipment retailer in town.

Get a bird's-eye view of the game at Safeco Field (right)

Seattle by Area

DOWNTOWN

SEATTLE CENTER, QUEEN ANNE HILL

CAPITOL HILL TO WASHINGTON PARK

UNIVERSITY DISTRICT

FREMONT, BALLARD, DISCOVERY PARK

FARTHER AFIELD

Downtown

Although it has always been the beating heart of Seattle's economy, Downtown is also home to cultural treasures. Here you'll find high-end hotels and restaurants, and scores of new condominium developments.

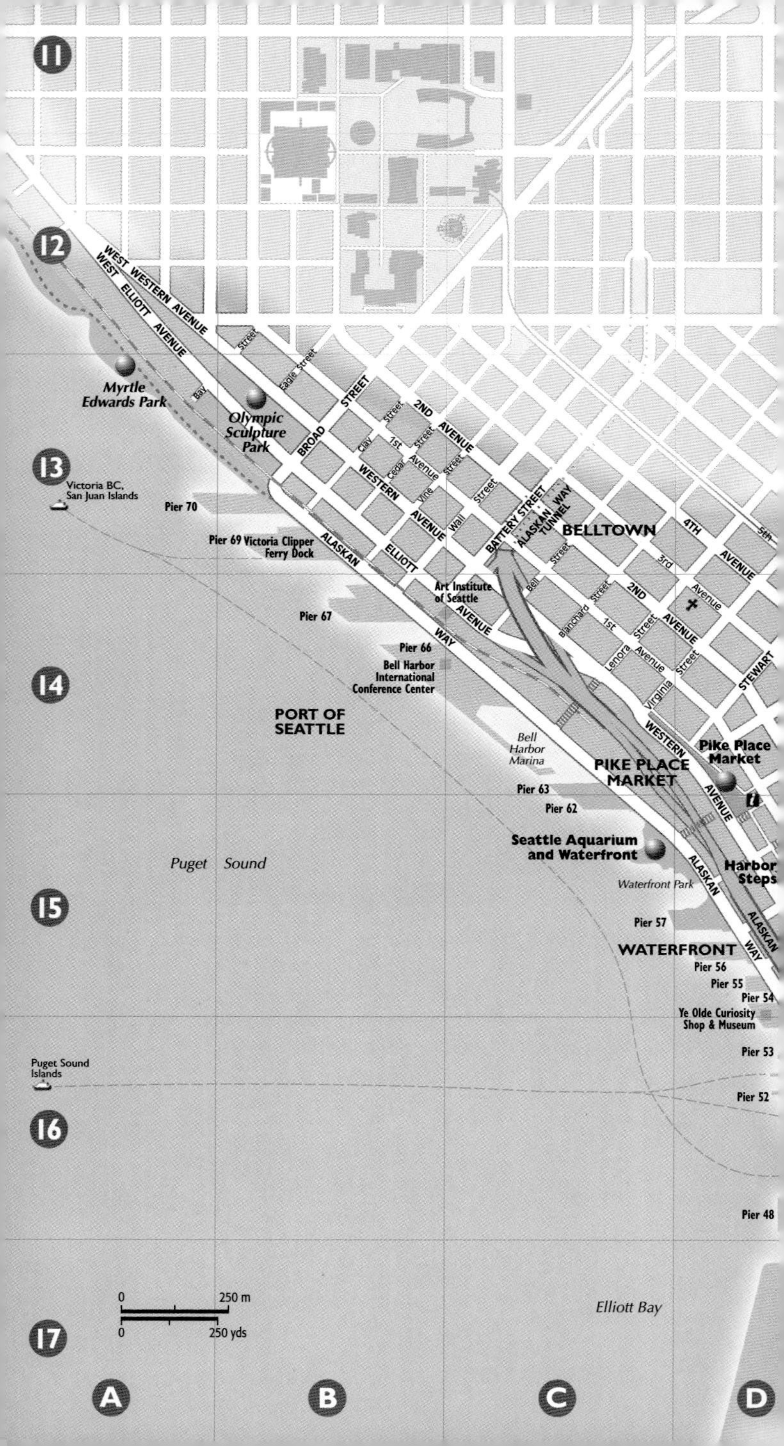
11
12
13
14
15
16
17
A
B
C
D
WEST WESTERN AVENUE
WEST ELLIOTT AVENUE
Myrtle Edwards Park
Olympic Sculpture Park
Bay
Street
Eagle Street
BROAD STREET
Clay Street
1st Avenue
Cedar Street
Vine Street
Wall Street
2ND AVENUE
WESTERN AVENUE
ELLIOTT AVENUE
ALASKAN WAY
BATTERY STREET
ALASKAN WAY TUNNEL
BELLTOWN
4TH AVENUE
5th
3rd Avenue
Bell Street
Blanchard Street
Lenora Street
Virginia Street
STEWART
Victoria BC, San Juan Islands
Pier 70
Pier 69
Victoria Clipper Ferry Dock
Art Institute of Seattle
Pier 67
Pier 66
Bell Harbor International Conference Center
PORT OF SEATTLE
Bell Harbor Marina
PIKE PLACE MARKET
Pike Place Market
Pier 63
Pier 62
Seattle Aquarium and Waterfront
Harbor Steps
Waterfront Park
Puget Sound
Pier 57
WATERFRONT
Pier 56
Pier 55
Pier 54
Ye Olde Curiosity Shop & Museum
Pier 53
Puget Sound Islands
Pier 52
Pier 48
0
250 m
0
250 yds
Elliott Bay

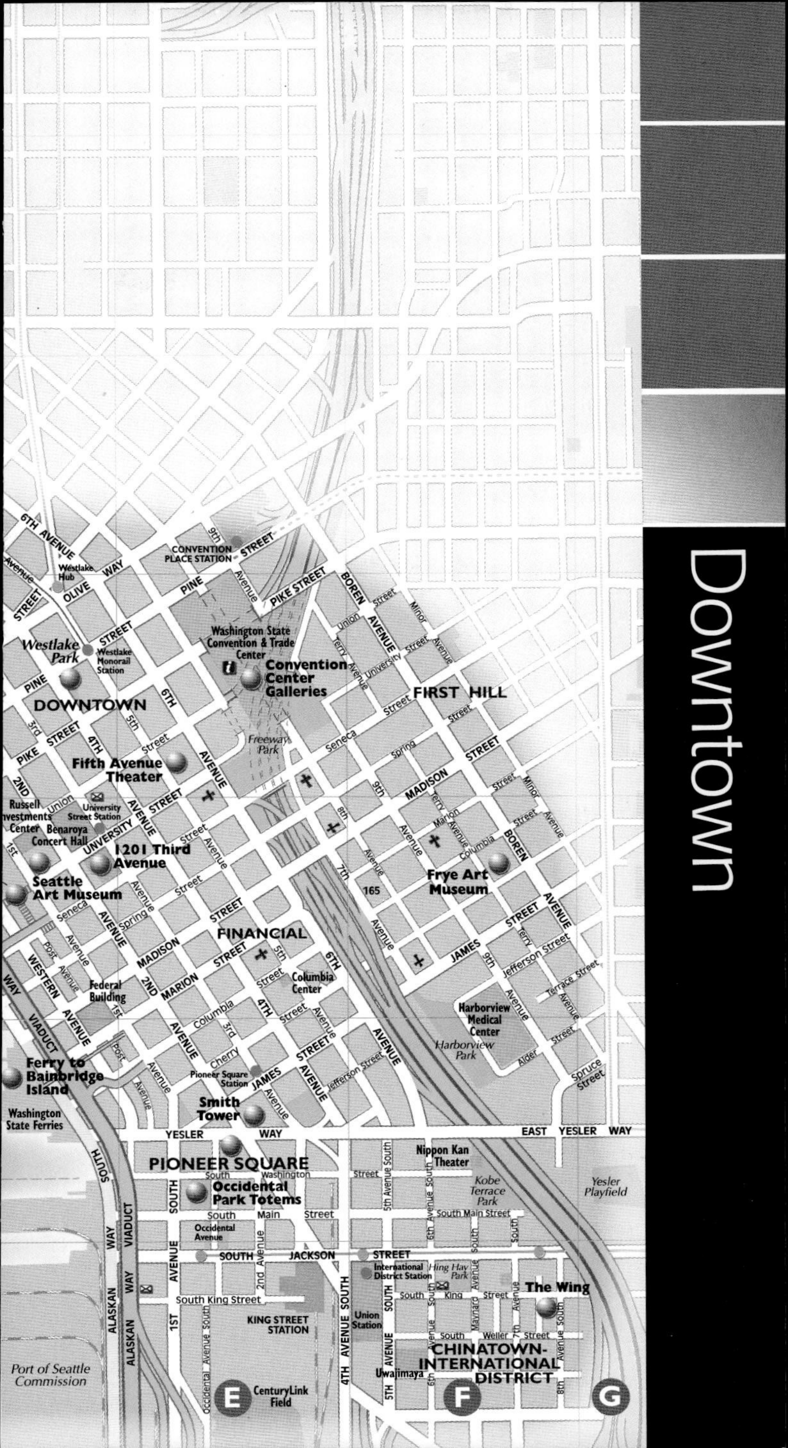

Downtown
6TH AVENUE
CONVENTION PLACE STATION
9th STREET
Westlake Hub
OLIVE WAY
PINE
PIKE STREET
BOREN AVENUE
Union Street
Minor Avenue
Washington State Convention & Trade Center
Westlake Park
Westlake Monorail Station
Convention Center Galleries
Terry Avenue
University Street
FIRST HILL
DOWNTOWN
6TH AVENUE
5th Street
3rd
4TH
Seneca
Spring
MADISON
Fifth Avenue Theater
Freeway Park
2ND
Russell Investments Center
Union
University Street Station
Benaroya Concert Hall
UNIVERSITY STREET
1201 Third Avenue
1st
Seattle Art Museum
Marion
Columbia
8th
7th
165
Frye Art Museum
FINANCIAL
JAMES
Jefferson Street
Terrace Street
Post
WESTERN
WAY
Federal Building
MARION
Columbia Center
Harborview Medical Center
Harborview Park
VIADUCT
Cherry
Alder
Spruce Street
Ferry to Bainbridge Island
Pioneer Square Station
Washington State Ferries
Smith Tower
YESLER WAY
EAST YESLER WAY
Nippon Kan Theater
PIONEER SQUARE
South Washington Street
5th Avenue South
6th Avenue South
Kobe Terrace Park
Yesler Playfield
Occidental Park Totems
South Main Street
Occidental Avenue
SOUTH
2nd Avenue
JACKSON STREET
International District Station
Hing Hay Park
The Wing
ALASKAN WAY VIADUCT
South King Street
Maynard Avenue
KING STREET STATION
Union Station
4TH AVENUE SOUTH
5TH AVENUE SOUTH
South Weller Street
CHINATOWN-INTERNATIONAL DISTRICT
Uwajimaya
8th Avenue South
Port of Seattle Commission
Occidental Avenue South
E
CenturyLink Field
F
G

Chinatown-International District

TOP 25

Eating out is one of the chief pleasures of Seattle's colorful Chinatown

THE BASICS

www.cidbia.org
F17
Between S Main and Lane streets and 5th and 8th avenues S; "Little Saigon" 12th Avenue S and Jackson Street
Central Link: International District-Chinatown

HIGHLIGHTS

- The many Asian restaurants
- The Wing museum
- Hing Hay Park, with its ornate pavilion and dragon mural
- Uwajimaya, a large Asian emporium

TIP

- If you're a karaoke fan, don't miss the scene at the Maekawa Bar, where Japanese food lends an authentic feel. Other neighborhood karaoke favorites include the Bush Garden and Fortune Sports Bar.

Bordered by the sparkling Union Station office park and two sports stadiums, Seattle's International District is home to the city's Chinese, Japanese, Filipino, Southeast Asian, Korean and other Asian communities.

Multicultural mix The first Asian people to arrive in Seattle were Chinese men, who moved north from California to build the railways. Anti-Chinese riots broke out in the 1880s and many Chinese were deported, only to return after 1889 to help rebuild the charred settlement. The Japanese arrived next, many establishing small farms and selling their goods at Pike Place Market (▷ 28) The Filipinos, the third group to arrive, now constitute Seattle's largest Asian community.

The neighborhood Smaller and more modest than San Francisco's Chinatown, the International District caters primarily to those who live and work in the neighborhood. Start your exploration at the fascinating and informative Wing museum (▷ 35). Before leaving the museum pick up a map of the neighborhood. Make sure you include Hing Hay Park and Uwajimaya, the largest Asian emporium in the Northwest.

Eating choices The district has many excellent Asian restaurants. Good bets include House of Hong, Shanghai Garden and Jade Garden. For Vietnamese food, head up to 12th and Jackson and try Tamarind Tree (▷ 44), or for Malaysian cuisine, check out Malay Satay Hut (▷ panel, 43) at 12th and Main.

The Bainbridge Island ferry (right) is one of several that ply the Sound (below)

Ferry to Bainbridge Island

There's nothing more delightful than catching a Washington State ferry to Bainbridge Island. Standing at the stern as the boat pulls away from Colman Dock, you can see the entire Seattle skyline unfold.

The ferry It takes 35 minutes to get to Bainbridge Island from the Downtown waterfront. En route, you can look back to see an amazing panorama: the Seattle cityscape and Mt. Rainier to the east, and Bainbridge Island and the snow-capped Olympic Range to the west.

Touring on foot Once you disembark at the Bainbridge ferry dock, walk the short distance to the town of Winslow, visit the charming boutiques, browse at Eagle Harbor Books, stop for lunch at Café Nola or order treats from the Bainbridge Vineyard. If it's Saturday (mid-Apr to mid-Nov), catch the market on the Winslow green, or on weekends visit Bainbridge's Island Winery for tasting. If you're synchronizing your return with the sunset, you could linger on the Waterfront Deck at the Harbor Public House.

Touring by car or bike If you have wheels, visit Bloedel Reserve and walk the trails (call in advance for reservations). Continuing across Agate Pass Bridge on to the Kitsap Peninsula, you enter Port Madison Indian Reservation and the town of Suquamish, where leader Chief Sealth is buried. The Squamish Museum gives an interesting insight into the tribe's history.

THE BASICS

Bainbridge Ferry
www.wsdot.wa.gov/ferries
D16
Colman Dock, pier 52; Alaskan Way and Marion Street
206/464-6400, 800/843-3779
From Seattle, 5.30am–1.35am; from Bainbridge, last ferry at 12.55am
Central Link to Pioneer Square
RapidRide C Line
Inexpensive

Bainbridge Vineyard
www.bainbridgevineyards.com
8989 Day Road E
206/842-9463
Tasting Sat–Sun 12–5. Tours some weekends

Bloedel Reserve
www.bloedelreserve.com
7521 NE Dolphin Drive
206/842-7631
Jun–Aug Tue–Wed 10–4, Thu–Sun 10–6; Sep–May Wed–Sun 10–4
Moderate

Olympic Sculpture Park TOP 25

Modern art on a grand scale along the waterfront, including Echo *(below right)*

THE BASICS

B13
Western Avenue
206/654–3100
Daily half hour before dawn to half hour after dusk
Taste Café, open late May–Aug, Sat–Sun
1, 2, 13, 15, 18, 21, 22 and many others
Free
Very good

Some of the Seattle Art Museum's most monumental and engaging sculptural works have been brought outdoors to greet the public in this waterfront park, transforming the former industrial waste-land into a stunning open-air gallery.

Birth of the park The idea for the park was born in the late 1990s, and finally came to fruition in 2007, thanks to a gift of $30 million from Mary and Jon Shirley, the latter a former president of Microsoft.

Innovative art One of the most prominent works in the collection is the pale, slender and dramatic 46ft (14m) tall *Echo*, by Spanish artist Jaume Piensa, installed in 2014. In the form of an elongated head, it towers over the entire waterfront. Other stand-out exhibits include the elegant, bright red *The Eagle* by American sculptor Alexander Calder, and Mark di Suvero's *Schubert Sonata*, its welded metal curves high-lighted by passing clouds. Also check out the fun series, *Eye Benches*, by Louise Bourgeois.

Neukom Vivarium American artist Mark Dion was commissioned by the Seattle Art Museum to create this mixed-media installation, which includes the 80ft (25m) long greenhouse that houses the exhibit's elements of sculpture, horticulture and the environment. Central to the exhibit is a felled tree, showing how it transforms as it decays, providing a habitat for insects, plants and bacteria.

HIGHLIGHTS

- *Echo*
- *The Eagle*
- Wandering among the curved forms of *Wake*, by Richard Serra
- *Seattle Cloud Cover*, on the footbridge, by Teresita Fernandez
- Viewing exhibits with the sunset as a backdrop

TIP

- Visitors are not allowed to touch or climb on the exhib-its, and bicycles, skateboards and rollerblades must not be used within the park.

A blend of ancient and modern in Pioneer Square (below)

TOP 25

Pioneer Square

Constructed after the Great Seattle Fire, Pioneer Square's brick buildings retain an architectural integrity you won't find elsewhere in the city.

From the ashes In 1852, Seattle's pioneers moved across Elliott Bay and built the first permanent settlement in what is now Pioneer Square. The area burned to the ground in 1889, but was quickly rebuilt. When gold was discovered in the Yukon, prospectors converged on Pioneer Square to board ships to Alaska, and the area became the primary outfitting post for miners.

Moving through the square Pioneer Square's most notable landmarks include Smith Tower (▷ 35), which has an observation deck, and the lovely glass-and-iron pergola at 1st and Yesler. Interesting stores line 1st Avenue south of Yesler. Walk through the lovely Grand Central Arcade, which opens onto Occidental Park (▷ 35), and cross Main Street, taking time to visit the Klondike Gold Rush National Historic Park.

Detours Take a short detour to enchanting Waterfall Park at 2nd and South Main; then backtrack to the bricked pedestrian walkway, and amble along the cobblestoned Occidental Place, taking time to explore the cluster of art galleries that extend around the corner to 1st and South Jackson. To end your exploration, dine at one of the area's excellent restaurants, catch some live music, or head for laughs at the Comedy Underground (▷ 40).

THE BASICS

Pioneer Square
www.pioneersquare.org
E16
Yesler Way to King Street and 2nd Avenue to Elliot Bay; visitor information booth in Occidental Square in summer

Klondike Gold Rush National Historic Park
www.nps.gov/klse/index.htm
319 2nd Avenue S
206/220–4240
Late May–early Sep daily 9–5; early Sep–late May 10–5
Lots of options to Pioneer Square Station
Central Link: Pioneer Square
Free

HIGHLIGHTS

- The pergola at 1st and Yesler
- Smith Tower
- Occidental Park and totem poles (▷ 35)
- Klondike Gold Rush National Historic Park
- Waterfall Park

Pike Place Market

TOP 25

HIGHLIGHTS

Market Arcade

- Stores: Read All About It (for newspapers), DiLaurenti's Grocery and Deli, Market Spice Teas, Tenzing Momo
- Restaurants: Athenian Inn, Sound View Café, Place Pigalle, Matt's in the Market

Sanitary Market Building/ Post Alley

- Stores: Jack's Fish Spot (▷ 43), Lamplight Books, Made in Washington (▷ 39)

TIP

- The information booth at 1st Avenue and Pike Street provides a useful map to find your way around.

To many residents, Pike Place Market is Seattle's heart and soul. Here, people of every background converge, from city professionals and farmers to hippie craftspeople and tourists.

Farmers' market Pike Place Market was founded in 1907 so that farmers could sell directly to the consumer and eliminate the middleman. It was an immediate success, and grew quickly until World War II precipitated a decline. Threatened by demolition in the 1960s, it underwent major renovation in 2012 and is protected as a Historic District.

Feast for the senses The three-block area stretching between Pike and Virginia has flowerstalls, fishsellers, produce displays, tea shops, bakeries, herbal apothecaries, magic stores and much more.

Looking for bargains—Pike Place Market is admired for its range of fresh fruit, vegetables and crab and seafood packed on ice; the central market building (bottom middle) is now a protected historic sight

Street musicians play Peruvian panpipes or sing the blues, and the fragrance of flowers and fresh bread fills the air. This is old Seattle frozen in time.

Exploring the market Before you start to explore, pick up a map from the information booth (1st Avenue and Pike Street, near the big clock) and head out from the bronze sculpture of Rachel the pig. Watch out for the flying fish (at Pike Place Fish), stop to admire the artfully arranged produce and flower displays, and make a sweep around the crafts area, where various handmade items are sold. Be sure to visit one of the earliest Starbucks locations at 1912 Pike Place. The shop opened way back in 1976, but it was actually the business's second location; the first store was opened in 1971 on Western Avenue. Still, it's steeped in caffeinated history.

THE BASICS

www.pikeplacemarket.org
D14
Between 1st Avenue and Western Avenue, Pike Street and Virginia Street
206/682–7453
Merchants daily 10–6, fresh produce from 7am, restaurants 6am–1.30am. Closed Christmas and Thanksgiving
Many buses, including Route 10 on Pine and 1st–4th avenues
Central Link: Westlake
Good

Seattle Aquarium and the Waterfront

TOP 25

HIGHLIGHTS

Aquarium

- Children's touch tidal pools
- Underwater dome room

Waterfront

- Bell Street complex restaurants and marina
- Seattle Great Wheel

Seattle's history and economic growth have been closely tied to the waterfront since 1853, when Henry Yesler built the first sawmill at the foot of the hill that bears his name.

Starting out When pioneers settled along Elliott Bay's eastern shores in 1852, the only flat land suitable for building was a narrow strip along the water, where 1st Avenue runs today. A century later, Seattle's landscape changed dramatically after a large expanse of Elliott Bay was reclaimed. Maritime industrial activity had moved south to pier 46 and below, and the Downtown waterfront was ripe for new beginnings.

Seattle Aquarium This is the place to acquaint yourself with Northwest marine life. In the

Meet sea otters at the Aquarium (left); fishermen statues atop a seafood restaurant on pier 66 (top middle); the Great Wheel by night (top right); watching the sealife of Puget Sound from the aquarium's underwater dome room (bottom right); welcome to pier 55 on the waterfront (bottom middle)

underwater dome room you can watch Puget Sound's "underworld" pass before your eyes. The Aquarium's newest exhibit is the 120,000-gal (454,000L) Window on Washington Waters, with a huge viewing window. Other highlights include the exceptional Pacific coral reef exhibit and, for children, the hands-on Discovery Lab.

The Waterfront Seattle's waterfront is getting a huge facelift, including replacing the seawall, removing the Alaskan Way Viaduct, remodeling streets and adding parks, paths and a cycle track. Involving 26 city blocks, the massive project should to be completed in 2019. Watching over all this activity is the most prominent new attraction, the Seattle Great Wheel. At 175ft (53m) high, it's one of the biggest Ferris wheels in the country, and offers superb views.

THE BASICS

Aquarium
www.seattleaquarium.org
C15
Pier 59: 1483 Alaskan Way at Pike Street
206/386-4300
Jul–Aug daily 9.30–7; Sep–Jun 9.30–5
Steamers Seafood Café
99
Very good
Expensive; reduction with CityPass

Waterfront
Alaskan Way between Broad (pier 70) and Main (pier 48)

Seattle Great Wheel
www. seattlegreatwheel.com
D15
1301 Alaskan Way
206/623-8607
Late Jun–late Sep daily 10am–11pm (midnight Fri–Sat); late Sep–late Jun Mon–Thu 11–10, Fri 11am–midnight, Sat 10am–midnight, Sun 10–10

Seattle Art Museum

TOP 25

HIGHLIGHTS

- Jonathan Borofsky's sculpture *Hammering Man*
- Indigenous art of Africa, Oceania and the Americas
- The Katherine White collection of African sculpture
- Pacific Northwest collection

TIP

- Admission is free on first Thu of month; visitors may also choose to pay what they can (permanent collections).

Some people love it; some can do without it. No one, however, fails to notice the imposing Seattle Art Museum or the 48ft (15m) black metal sculpture that dominates its entrance.

Another world The steel-and-glass-fronted structure of the Seattle Art Museum (SAM), opened in 1991 and expanded in 2008, steps up the hill between 1st and 2nd avenues. To reach the galleries, you ascend a grand staircase, walking the gauntlet between monumental paired rams, guardian figures and sacred camels from the Ming dynasty.

Dazzling collections SAM's permanent collections range from the indigenous art of Africa, Oceania and the Americas to modern US

The Hammering Man, *Jonathan Borofsky, 1991 (left); Native American art, and further galleries with art from Oceania and Africa (top and bottom middle); Modern and Contemporary Galleries, with* Importune: Stage 1 *by Cai Guo-Qiang (right)*

paintings and sculpture. Other galleries feature European exhibitions from the Medieval period through the 19th century. A Northwest Coast collection features large pieces, including four full-scale carved Kwakiutl houseposts. In other galleries, the museum presents traveling exhibitions and launches major shows of its own. Recent exhibitions have featured modernism in the Pacific Northwest, nature and pattern in Japanese design, and paintings and drawings of the European avant-garde.

Hammering Man Of the 48ft (15m) sculpture out front, sculptor Jonathan Borofsky has said: "I want this work to appeal to all people of Seattle—not just artists, but families young and old. At its heart, society reveres the worker. The *Hammering Man* is the worker in all of us."

THE BASICS

www.seattleartmuseum.org
D15
1300 1st Avenue
206/654–3100
Wed–Sun 10–5 (Thu until 9). Closed some public holidays
Taste
10, 29, 41, 47, 71
Central Link: University Street
Very good
Expensive; half-price with CityPass; free for those over 62. Admission ticket also includes the Downtown museum and Asian Art Museum in Volunteer Park.

More to See

1201 THIRD AVENUE

As critics lambasted this late 1980s Kohn Pederson Fox building as an Empire State clone, the public applauded the postmodern style as relief from the cold glass boxes that dominate Downtown.

E15 | 1201 3rd Avenue

CONVENTION CENTER GALLERIES

www.wscc.com

The North Galleria has an outstanding collection featuring Northwest painting, sculpture, ceramic and glass art.

E14 | 800 Convention Place | 206/694–5000 | Daily 7am–10pm | Central Link: Westlake

FIFTH AVENUE THEATER

www.5thavenue.org

Built in 1926, this ornately carved theater is patterned after the imperial throne room in Beijing's Forbidden City.

E14 | 1308 5th Avenue | 206/625–1900 | 101

FRYE ART MUSEUM

www.fryemuseum.org

This beautiful, spacious gallery devoted to representational art rotates works from the permanent collection, most notably pieces by William Merritt Chase, Winslow Homer, John Singer Sargeant and Renoir.

F15 | 704 Terry Avenue | 206/622–9250 | Tue–Sun 11–5 (Thu until 7) | Café | 3, 4 or 12 (on 3rd Avenue) | Excellent | Free | Sun afternoon concerts, films, workshops and lectures

HARBOR STEPS

In creating a pedestrian link between the Waterfront and 1st Avenue, Vancouver architect Arthur Anderson crafted an inviting urban plaza which is a very pleasant spot to relax.

D15 | University Avenue | 99

MYRTLE EDWARDS PARK

With a pedestrian and bicycle path along the shore of Elliott Bay, this urban park has some of the best mountain and Sound views in the city.

A13 | 3130 Alaskan Way West | 33

Inside the beautiful Fifth Avenue Theater

OCCIDENTAL PARK TOTEMS

Duane Pasco's painted cedar logs—*Sun and Raven*, *Tsonqua* and *Killer Whale and Bear*—standing proud in Occidental Park date from 1975.

E16 Occidental Park, Occidental Avenue S and S Main in Pioneer Square 99

SMITH TOWER

www.smithtower.com

When it opened in 1914, Smith Tower was Seattle's first steel-framed skyscraper and the tallest building outside of New York City. At 42 stories, it remained the tallest building west of the Mississippi until 1969. For a modest fee, you can ride to the 35th floor in the company of the last of Seattle's elevator attendants to get a sweeping view of Downtown.

E16 506 2nd Avenue and Yesler Way Observation deck May–Sep daily 10–7; Oct–Apr 10–5 Inexpensive

WESTLAKE PARK

With its potted plants, fountain and colorful furniture, this pleasant little plaza in the heart of Downtown is a good place to take a break from shopping or perhaps enjoy an outdoor concert. You can even play ping-pong here, and there's a bright pink piano for public use. It's also known as a venue for protests.

D14 Monorail from Seattle Center; Central Link to Westlake Station.

THE WING

www.wingluke.org

A fine example of Seattle's rich Asian and Pacific Island heritage, the Wing Luke Museum of the Asian Pacific Experience includes permanent exhibits such as "Our Roots Run Deep and Broad," a moving portrayal of one immigrant's cultural heritage.

F17 719 S King Street 206/623-5124 Tue–Sun 10–5 (until 8 on 1st Thu and 3rd Sat of month) 7 and 14 to Maynard and Jackson, 36 and bus tunnel (International District Station), 99 Central Link: Chinatown-International District Moderate

Family beachcombing at Myrtle Edwards Park

Smith Tower, one of the buildings in Pioneer Square

Downtown Stroll

Dive into the city's hectic center, visiting the famed Pike Place Market, the Waterfront, Pioneer Square and the entertaining retail core.

DISTANCE: 2.8 miles (4km) **ALLOW:** 1.5 hours

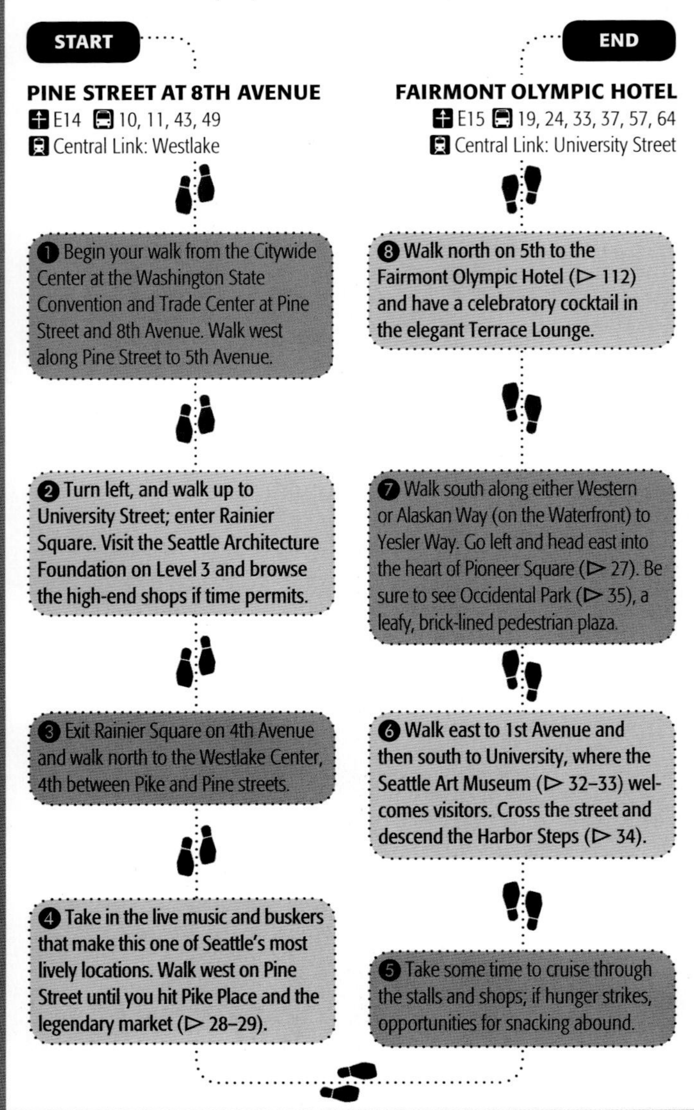

START

PINE STREET AT 8TH AVENUE

E14 10, 11, 43, 49

Central Link: Westlake

1 Begin your walk from the Citywide Center at the Washington State Convention and Trade Center at Pine Street and 8th Avenue. Walk west along Pine Street to 5th Avenue.

2 Turn left, and walk up to University Street; enter Rainier Square. Visit the Seattle Architecture Foundation on Level 3 and browse the high-end shops if time permits.

3 Exit Rainier Square on 4th Avenue and walk north to the Westlake Center, 4th between Pike and Pine streets.

4 Take in the live music and buskers that make this one of Seattle's most lively locations. Walk west on Pine Street until you hit Pike Place and the legendary market (▷ 28–29).

5 Take some time to cruise through the stalls and shops; if hunger strikes, opportunities for snacking abound.

6 Walk east to 1st Avenue and then south to University, where the Seattle Art Museum (▷ 32–33) welcomes visitors. Cross the street and descend the Harbor Steps (▷ 34).

7 Walk south along either Western or Alaskan Way (on the Waterfront) to Yesler Way. Go left and head east into the heart of Pioneer Square (▷ 27). Be sure to see Occidental Park (▷ 35), a leafy, brick-lined pedestrian plaza.

8 Walk north on 5th to the Fairmont Olympic Hotel (▷ 112) and have a celebratory cocktail in the elegant Terrace Lounge.

END

FAIRMONT OLYMPIC HOTEL

E15 19, 24, 33, 37, 57, 64

Central Link: University Street

Shopping

AGATE DESIGNS

www.agatedesigns.com
Come here for jewelry, glittering minerals, ornaments and lamps made from agate.
E16 120 1st Avenue S
206/621-3063
Mon–Sat 10–5, Sun 11–4

ALHAMBRA

www.alhambrastyle.com
Sophisticated clothing, from dainty silk dresses to velvet yoga pants, for women. Live jazz Saturday afternoons entertains while you shop.
D14 101 Pine Street
206/621-9571 Mon–Sat 10–6.30, Sun 11.30–6

ANN TAYLOR

www.anntaylor.com
Classic lines and easy elegance in women's fashions, ranging from career to informal wear.
E14 600 Pine Street
206/652-0663
Mon–Sat 10–7, Sun 11–7

ANTHROPOLOGIE

www.anthropologie.com
Retro-inspired women's clothing, accessories and home furnishings that are undeniably elegant.
D14 1513 5th Avenue
206/381-5900
Mon–Sat 10–8, Sun 11–6

AZUMA GALLERY

Japanese art, including old and new prints, paintings, screens, folk art and ceramics.
E17 530 1st Avenue S
206/622-5599
Tue–Sat 11–5.30

BABY & CO.

www.babyandco.us
Pricey, whimsical clothes for adventurous women.
D14 1936 1st Avenue
206/448-4077 Mon–Sat 10–6, Sun 12–5

BANANA REPUBLIC

Clean and austere urban stylings for men and women. Casual and formal wear in the former Coliseum Theater.
D14 500 Pike Street
206/622-2303 Mon–Fri 10–8, Sat 10–9, Sun 11–6

BARNEYS

www.barneys.com
Chic and trendy for that minimalist New York style. Prada and other popular designers.
E14 600 Pine Street
206/622-6300
Mon–Sat 10–9, Sun 11–7

BCBG

www.bcbg.com
Beautiful evening gowns, career and casual creations by Paris designer Max Azria.
D14 600 Pine Street
206/447-3400 Mon–Sat 9.30–8, Sun 11–6

TASTES OF SEATTLE

What better way to elicit the flavor of the region than to take back a salmon and a bottle of Washington wine. Fishsellers at the Pike Place Market will pack fresh salmon on ice to travel and many fish markets and gift stores like "Made in Washington" carry gift boxes of smoked salmon that do not require refrigeration.

BELLA UMBRELLA

www.bellaumbrella.com
If the west-coast weather catches you unawares, you'll find a stylish solution in this chic umbrella store. They have parasols, too, should the sun get too much.
D12 1535 1st Avenue
206/297-1540
Mon–Sat 10–6, Sun 11–5

BROOKS BROTHERS

Superior men's clothing in traditional styles.
E14 1330 5th Avenue
206/624-4400 Mon–Fri 9.30–7, Sat 10–6, Sun 12–5

BUTCH BLUM

Fine European fashions for men and women; featured designers include Giorgio Armani, Luciano Barbera and Stella McCartney.
E14 1332 6th Avenue
206/622-5760
Mon–Sat 10–6

CHICOS

www.chicos.com
Distinctive and fun women's clothes with attitude that travel easily. Mostly wash-and-wear.
E14 600 Pine Street
206/624-5549 Mon–Sat 10–8, Sun 11–7

EARTH, WIND & FIRE

www.earthwindandfire-boutique.com
Women's boutique selling stylish, handmade apparel

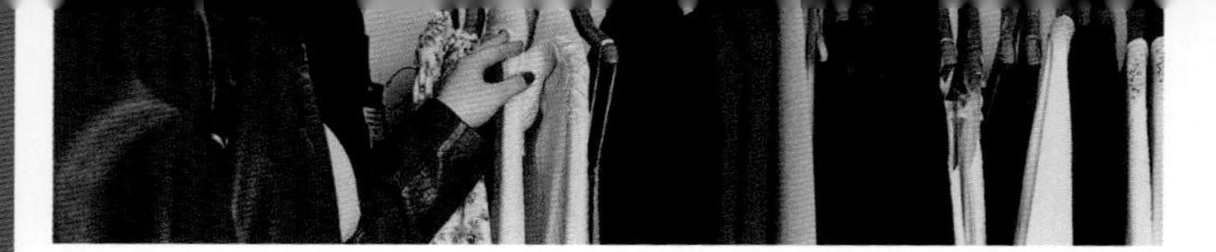

including outer-wear for braving any bad weather with flair.
H13 1514 Pike Place #13 206/383–2153 or 206/448–2529 Daily 10–6

EDDIE BAUER
www.eddiebauer.com
Casual wear and accessories for men and women with an outdoor lifestyle.
E14 600 Pine Street 206/622–2766 Mon–Sat 10–9, Sun 11–7

EILEEN FISHER
www.eileenfisher.com
Simple yet elegant apparel for the professional woman of 30 to 65.
D14 525 Pine Street 206/748–0770 Mon–Sat 10–6, Sun 12–5

ENDLESS KNOT
www.endlessknotseattle.com
Elegant and original women's clothes.
C14 2300 1st Avenue 206/448–0355 Mon–Wed 10–8, Thu–Sat 10–9, Sun 10–7

FACERE JEWELRY ART
www.facerejewelryart.com
One-of-a-kind Victorian and contemporary jewelry.
E14 1420 5th Avenue 206/624–6768 Mon–Sat 10–6

FILSON
www.filson.com
High-quality outdoor clothing for men is both made and sold here. You can also get luggage, briefcases, travel kits and accessories.
Off map 1555 4th Avenue S 206/622–3147 Mon–Sat 10–6, Sun 12–5

FLANAGAN & LANE ANTIQUES
www.flanagan-laneantiques.com
A treasure house of antiques, including furniture, paintings, porcelain, jewelry, silver and books.
E17 165 S Jackson Street 206/682–0098 Mon–Sat 11–5, Sun 12–5

FLURY & CO. GALLERY
www.fluryco.com
Vintage photographs of Native American life; Native American objects, beadwork and carvings.
E16 322 1st Avenue S 206/587–0260 Mon–Sat 11–5.30

FOX'S GEM SHOP
www.foxgemshop.com
Fine jewelry since 1912. Expensive.
E14 1341 5th Avenue 206/623–2528 Mon–Sat 10–6

GLASSHOUSE STUDIO
www.glasshouse-studio.com
The Northwest's oldest glass-blowing studio has a team of glass artists producing beautiful pieces, sold–along with the work of 40 other artists–in their adjacent store.
E17 311 Occidental Avenue S 206/682–9939 Mon–Sat 10–5, Sun 11–4; glass-blowing demonstrations Mon–Sat 10–11.30 and 1–5

GALLERY WALKS

On the first Thursday of the month, Pioneer Square galleries and those in the Pike Place Market area open into the evening for the monthly art walk. Many galleries take this opportunity to preview their new shows.

GREG KUCERA GALLERY
www.gregkucera.com
Watch out for this top city gallery.
E16 212 3rd Avenue S 206/624–0770 Tue–Sat 10.30–5.30, Sun 1–5

ISADORA'S
www.isadoras.com
Antique and vintage jewelry ranges from Georgian to mid-20th-century pieces. Prices start at around $90 and go up, and up, and up.
D14 1601 1st Avenue, corner of Pine Street 206/441–7711 or 855/663–0672 Mon–Sat 11–6, Sun 11–5

J. CREW
www.jcrew.com
Stylish, casual wear for men and women, with the emphasis on natural fibers and comfort.
E14 600 Pine Street 206/652–9788 Mon–Sat 10–8, Sun 11–7

KUHLMAN
www.kuhlmanseattle.com
A trendsetting men's and women's boutique that

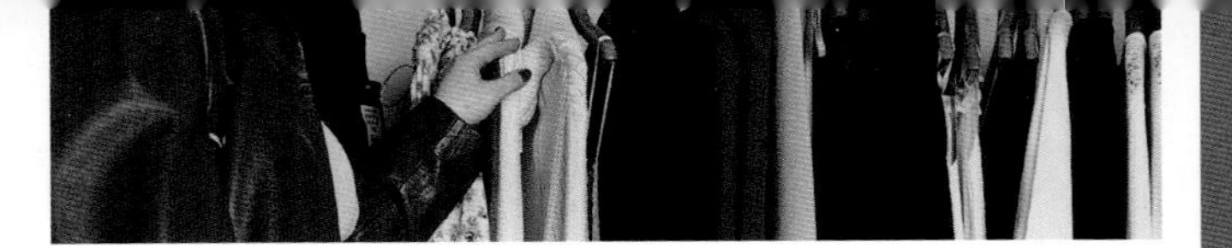

specializes in tailor-made, unique pieces for Seattle's young professionals.
C13 2419 1st Avenue 206/441-1999 Mon–Sat 11–7, Sun 12–6

THE LEGACY

Seattle's oldest and finest gallery for Northwest Native American and Inuit art and objects. Founded in 1933.
D15 1003 1st Avenue 206/624-6350 Tue–Sat 11–5.30

MADE IN WASHINGTON

Handicrafts, foods and wines from the region. Shipping available.
D14 1530 Post Alley 206/467-0788 Daily 10–6

MAGIC MOUSE

Fanciful, high-end toys for kids of all ages.
E16 603 1st Avenue 206/682-8097 Mon–Sat 10–7

MARIO'S

Fashionable Downtown store specializing in clean, classic lines and featuring designers like Donna Karan and Giorgio Armani.
E14 1513 6th Avenue 206/223-1461 Mon–Sat 10–6, Sun 12–5

MARKET MAGIC SHOP

Supplies for budding young magicians to pros.
D14 1st level below the food stalls, Pike Place Market 206/624-4271 Daily 10–5

NORDSTROM

This venerable institution stocks clothing and shoes for the entire family.
E14 500 Pine Street 206/628-2111 Mon–Sat 9.30–9, Sun 10–7

NORTHWEST WOODWORKERS GALLERY

Local artists' cooperative that exhibits phenomenal craftsmanship and design.
Off map 211 1st Avenue 206/625-0542 Tue–Fri 10–6, Sat–Sun 10–5

PATAGONIA

State-of-the-art outdoor clothing for adults and children.
C14 2100 1st Avenue 206/622-9700 Mon–Sat 10–6 (until 7 Fri), Sun 11–5

PHOENIX RISING GALLERY

Fine crafts gallery in the north end of the Market showcasing beautiful and original jewelry, ceramics and glassware.
D14 2030 Western Avenue (in the Pike Place Market) 206/728-2332 Daily 10–6

SEATTLE MYSTERY BOOKSHOP

www.seattlemystery.com
A very personalized independent bookstore that specializes in... well, that's no mystery. It has a great selection, knowledgeable staff and lots of author events.
E16 117 Cherry Street 206/587-5737 Mon 10–5, Tue–Sat 10–6, Sun 12–5

SWAY & CAKE

Trendy women's boutique loaded with denim, stylish tees and cutting-edge accessories.
E14 1631 6th Avenue 206/624-2699 Mon–Wed 10–7, Thu–Sat 10–8, Sun 11–6

TRAVER GALLERY

Contemporary painting, sculpture and ceramics by major artists. The gallery is also a leading dealer in contemporary studio glass.
D15 110 Union, 2nd floor 206/587-6501 Tue–Fri 10–6, Sat 10–5, Sun 12–5

WORLD SPICE MERCHANTS

www.worldspice.com
It's worth coming here just for the aroma, but the huge selection of spices, teas and original blends are not to be sniffed at. They also sell pepper mills, grinders, jars and cookbooks.
D15 1509 Western Avenue, by Pike Place market 206/682-7274

WOVEN ART

www.wovenartseattle.com
Beautiful hand-knotted rugs are imported from the Middle East, China, India and Pakistan.
E16 200 1st Avenue S 206/340-4011 Mon–Sat 10–6, Sun 11–5

Entertainment and Nightlife

ACT – A CONTEMPORARY THEATRE
www.acttheatre.org
A wide-ranging and full program of performances in the five theaters here includes drama, musicals, dance, comedy, cabaret.
E14 700 Union Street
206/292–7660; box office 206/292–7676

BALTIC ROOM
This trendy lounge features live music—mostly piano jazz—stiff drinks and a Wednesday "jungle night." Dancing, too.
F13 1207 Pine Street
206/625–4444

BLACK BOTTLE
This self-described "gastro-tavern" serves gourmet dishes at reasonable prices. Later in the evening, it turns into one of Belltown's coolest spots.
C13 2600 1st Avenue
206/441–1500

COMEDY UNDERGROUND
www.comedyunderground.com
National and local comedy acts with audience participation. Located under Swannie's Restaurant.
E16 109 Washington Street 206/628–0303

THE CROCODILE
www.thecrocodile.com
The hippest local and national touring bands play here at this birthplace of grunge, previously co-owned by REM guitarist Peter Buck.
C13 2200 2nd Avenue
206/441–4618

DIMITRIOU'S JAZZ ALLEY
www.jazzalley.com
Legendary jazz performers in a pleasant setting. Dinner before ensures a good seat.
D13 2033 6th Avenue
206/441–9729

EL GAUCHO PAMPAS ROOM
Jazz supper club open Friday and Saturday nights. Round tables, understated lighting, a large dance floor and a large stage. Cabaret-style entertainment.
C13 2505 1st Avenue
206/728–1140

FENIX
www.fenixunderground.com
A new "Fenix" rose from the rubble after earthquake damage destroyed the club. Live music, from rock to world music.
E16 101 S Washington Street 206/405–4323

TICKETS

Ticket/Ticket sells remaining tickets for music, dance, theater and comedy venues at half-price on the day of the show. Only cash is accepted in payment. There are two locations; one at Pike Place Market and the other on Broadway E (▷ 119).

FIFTH AVENUE THEATER
This historic, ornate hall hosts new productions of classic musicals and touring Broadway shows.
E14 1308 5th Avenue
206/625–1900

FIRESIDE ROOM
With its overstuffed chairs and fireplace, this spot in the stately Sorrento Hotel takes you back to earlier, more genteel times.
F15 900 Madison Street 206/622–6400

FRYE MUSEUM CONCERT SERIES
Free Sunday afternoon chamber music concerts at 2pm roughly once a month at the Frye.
F15 704 Terry Avenue
206/622–9250

HIGHWAY 99 BLUES CLUB
www.highway99blues.com
Top-class blues acts play in an intimate setting with a great old-timey atmosphere. Get there early for a good seat—lots of pillars block sightlines from some areas. Good Southern food too.
D15 1414 Alaskan Way, across from the Aquarium 206/382–2171
Wed–Thu 6pm–1am, Fri 4pm–2am, Sat 6pm–2am

KELL'S IRISH RESTAURANT & PUB
The elegance of a Dublin supper room and the warmth of an Irish pub. Irish music.

D14 1916 Post Alley
206/728–1916

NEW ORLEANS CREOLE RESTAURANT
Cajun zydeco and jazz in Pioneer Square.
E16 114 1st Avenue S
206/622–2563

NORTHWEST ASIAN-AMERICAN THEATER
The Northwest's only Asian-American theater mounts productions in the International District.
F17 409 7th Avenue S at Jackson 206/340–1449

PARAMOUNT THEATER
www.paramount.com
Seattle's premiere main-stage for the concert tours of superstars and for traveling musical theater productions. Built in 1928 as a silent film and vaudeville house, it has been beautifully restored.
E13 911 Pine Street
206/682–1414

THE PIKE PUB & BREWERY
Popular for its good food, excellent craft beers and affordable prices.
D15 1415 1st Avenue (in the Market) 206/622-6044 Until midnight

QUEEN CITY GRILL
Belltown's classiest pub. The first-rate kitchen specializes in grilled entrées. Crowded and noisy.
C14 2201 1st Avenue
206/443–0975

SAFECO FIELD
www.seattlemariners.com
The Seattle Mariners play at this "state-of-the-art" ballpark. The open-air stadium seats 47,000 and has a retractable roof. Baseball season runs from spring into fall; Safeco tours are available year-round.
Off map 1250 1st Avenue S at Royal Brougham
206/346–4287 for tickets

TAVOLÀTA
This industrial yet homey restaurant and bar serves an incredible menu of Italian classics, but it's also one of the most visually stunning bars in Belltown. A place to see and be seen.
C13 2323 2nd Avenue
206/838–8008

OUTDOOR CONCERTS

In summer, Seattleites enjoy several outdoor concert series, including:

- Out-to-Lunch noontime "brown bag" concerts at various Downtown locations.
- BECU ZooTunes, a summer-long outdoor concert series hosted by the Woodland Park Zoo. A perennial favorite of locals. Past performers include Indigo Girls, the Herbie Hancock Trio and Bela Fleck.

5500 Phinney Avenue North 206/548–2400; www.zoo.org/zootunes

TEATRO ZINZANNI
This three-hour theater/food extravaganza features an unparalleled comedic cabaret act and food created by Seattle celebrity chef Tom Douglas.
B11 222 Mercer Street
206/802–0015

THEATERSPORTS
Improvisational drama evenings at the Market Theater.
E15 1428 Post Alley at the Pike Street Market
206/587–2414 Fri, Sat at 10pm, Sun at 7pm

VICEROY
Decked out in 1960s-era chic—a stuffed boar's head and bottomless leather sofas. A can't-miss spot for hipness fans.
C13 2332 2nd Avenue
206/956–VICE (8423)

VIRGINIA INN
A Seattle institution. Art on the walls and a posted quotation providing food for thought for an eclectic group of patrons.
C14 1937 1st Avenue
206/728–1937 Sun–Thu 11.30am–midnight, Fri–Sat 11.30am–2am

VON'S GRAND CITY CAFÉ
The city's best martini "or your money back." Prime rib and fruitwood-smoked turkey stand out in this dark-wood haunt papered with quirky memorabilia.
E14 1225 1st Avenue
206/621–8667

Restaurants

PRICES

Prices are approximate, based on a 3-course meal for one person.
$$$ over $50
$$ $30–$50
$ under $30

ARAGONA ($$)
www.aragonaseattle.com
Upscale and imaginative Spanish cuisine— choose small plates or regular entrées. Great cocktails.
D15 96 Union Street
206/682–3590
Dinner Mon–Sat

BAUHAUS ($)
Stylish coffee bar and bookstore offering choice people-watching and selling pastries and wraps.
F13 301 E Pine Street
206/625–1600
Mon– Fri 6am–1am, Sat 7am–1am, Sun 8am–1am

BROOKLYN SEAFOOD, STEAK & OYSTER BAR ($$$)
The perfect place for slurping cool oysters and sipping ice-cool Martinis.
E15 1212 2nd Avenue
206/224–7000 Lunch Mon–Sat, dinner nightly

CAFÉ CAMPAGNE ($$)
Dim and warm, this cozy spot in the Pike Place Market is perfect for a glass of wine. Sunday brunch is one of the best.
D14 1600 Post Alley
206/728–2233
Lunch and dinner daily, brunch on weekends

THE CRAB POT ($$$)
The waterfront location and come-as-you-are appeal is perfect for families. Don a bib and crack your crab right on the paper-lined tables.
D15 1301 Alaskan Way (pier 57) 206/624–1890
Lunch and dinner daily

CUTTERS ($$)
Family-friendly seafood dining at the north end of Pike Place Market.
C14 2001 Western Avenue 206/448–4884
Lunch and dinner daily, brunch Sun

DAHLIA LOUNGE ($$$)
Innovative cuisine in colorful surroundings.
D14 2001 4th Avenue
206/682–4142 Lunch Mon–Fri, dinner nightly

FARESTART

This nonprofit restaurant serves delicious, hearty meals at budget prices while training homeless men and women for jobs in the food service industry. The weekday lunch buffet, which includes a range of remarkably ambitious preparations, is popular and on Thursday nights top chefs from local restaurants prepare outstanding dinners. There's a fixed price for full-course meals and all proceeds go back into the program.
www.farestart.org
D14 700 Virginia Street 206/267-7601
Lunch Mon–Fri, dinner Thu only

DRAGONFISH ASIAN CAFÉ ($)
A fun eatery with lively appetizers and specialty martinis, in the heart of the hotel district.
E14 722 Pine Street
206/467–7777
Lunch and dinner daily

ETTA'S SEAFOOD ($$)
Just outside Pike Place Market, restaurateur Tom Douglas's ode to seafood with an Asian, innovative bent is a favorite with the crowds.
C14 2020 Western Avenue 206/443–6000
Lunch and dinner daily, brunch on weekends

FLYING FISH ($$)
Hip, stylish, approachable and always packed. Expect unusual fish and fun preparation: Don't miss the family-style fish tacos.
C14 300 Westlake Avenue 206/728–8595
Dinner daily

FROLIK ($$)
www.motifseattle.com
As fun as the name implies, this super-modern dining hot spot in the Motif hotel has a really cool 5th-floor patio and chic, intimate spaces inside. Cuisine is modern American.
E14 1415 5th Avenue 206/971–8015
Breakfast, lunch and dinner daily

IVAR'S ($$)
Ask anyone for fish and chips in Seattle and they'll send you to Ivar's. The casual fish bars are ideal for an easy lunch.
D15 1001 Alaskan Way (Pier 54) 206/624-6852
Lunch and dinner daily

JACK'S FISH SPOT ($)
Locals know this is the place to go for great *cioppino* and fresh fish 'n' chips.
D14 1514 Pike Place Market 206/467-0514
Lunch daily

LOULAY $$$
www.thechefinthehat.com
Chef Thierry Rautureau uses the freshest local ingredients for his very French menus in this classy restaurant.
E14 600 Union Street 206/402-4588
Breakfast, lunch and dinner daily

MACHIAVELLI ($$)
Casual and inexpensive; tasty pastas served on tables laid with checkered tablecloths.
F13 1215 Pine Street
206/621-7941
Dinner Mon–Sat

MACRINA BAKERY ($)
Freshly baked breads and pastries, and shots of espresso greet sleepy urbanites. Freshly pre-pared daily "special" sandwiches and soups.
C14 2408 1st Avenue
206/448-4032
Daily 7am–6pm

MAMA'S MEXICAN KITCHEN ($)
The funky crowds of Belltown head here for inexpensive Mexican fare and to sip cocktails amid the kitschy decor.
C13 2234 2nd Avenue
206/728-6262
Lunch and dinner daily

MANEKI ($$)
An International District standby, founded in 1923. Stellar sushi only made better by out-standing service.
F16 304 6th Avenue S
206/622-2631
Dinner Tue–Sun

MATT'S IN THE MARKET ($$$)
This intimate café boasts the best menu—and the best location—of any restaurant in the Pike Place area.
D14 94 Pike Street, Suite 32 206/467-7909
Lunch and dinner Mon–Sat

THE METROPOLITAN GRILL ($$$)
Stellar steaks and legen-dary martinis draw crowds nightly. Happy hour features inexpensive food specials in the bar, where stogies are encouraged.
E16 820 2nd Avenue
206/624-3287 Lunch Mon–Fri, dinner nightly

MALAY SATAY HUT

Tasty authentic Malaysian food has locals lining up nightly for a daring taste of something different.
www.malaysatayhut.com
G16 212 12th Avenue S 206/324-4091
Lunch and dinner Wed–Mon

OHANA ($)
This Belltown eatery offers delicious Asian food with a Hawaiian twist, served in a funky, faux-tropical setting. Cocktails; sushi bar.
C14 2207 1st Avenue
206/956-9329
Mon 5pm–2am, Tue–Sun 11.30am–2am

PALACE KITCHEN ($$)
Palace Kitchen offers urban American dining at its best. High ceilings and dim lighting make the uniform-clad cooks in the open kitchen even more fun to watch.
D13 2030 5th Avenue
206/448-2001 Lunch Mon–Fri, dinner nightly

PANAMA HOTEL TEA & COFFEE HOUSE ($)
This International District café serves up more than 20 varieties of tea: In a building that was once a Japanese bathhouse, a window in the floor provides a glimpse at its former history, including belongings left behind by Japanese-Americans who were rounded up and sent to internment camps during World War II.
F16 605 S Main Street
206/515-4000
Mon–Sat 8am–10pm, Sun 9am–8pm

LE PICHET ($$)

Café au lait in the morning, baguettes at lunch and *charcuterie* and ever-changing specials at night make for casual French café dining at its best.

D14 1933 1st Avenue 206/256–1499 Breakfast daily, lunch and dinner Thu–Sun

PIKE PLACE CHOWDER ($)

www.pikeplacechowder.com

Three-time winner of the prestigious "Nation's Best Chowder" title, this place serves chowder in several styles (including vegan).

D14 1530 Post Alley 206/267–2537 Lunch and dinner daily

PINK DOOR ($$)

Located in Post Alley, this intimate Italian bistro has an outdoor deck with great views of Elliott Bay. An eclectic array of cabaret performers entertain most nights of the week.

D14 1919 Post Alley 206/443–3241 Lunch and dinner daily

RESTAURANT ZOE ($$)

Set in the heart of Seattle's hip Belltown neighborhood, young, beautiful and discerning diners pack the room for expertly prepared fish and seafood, and fun cocktails.

C14 1318 E Union Street 206/256–2060 Dinner daily

SALUMI ($)

www.salumicuredmeats.com

Seattleites flock to this little lunch spot for the great cured meat platters and sandwiches. Come early, or call ahead for a take-out to avoid the long line of devoted regulars.

E16 309 3rd Avenue S 206/621–8772 Lunch Tue–Fri

SERIOUS PIE ($$)

Tom Douglas's newest venture serves authentic and tasty brick-oven pizza and a full menu of beer, wine and cocktails in a delightfully publike space.

D14 316 Virginia Street 206/838–7388 Lunch and dinner daily

TAMARIND TREE ($)

A standout Vietnamese restaurant in the heart of Little Saigon. A warm, romantic atmosphere and an authentic menu draw crowds from all parts of the city.

G16 1036 S Jackson Street, Suite A 206/860–1404 Lunch and dinner daily

SEATTLE BAGEL BAKERY

Don't miss this first-rate bagel stop. Order "to go" for a picnic outside, on the Harbor Steps.

D15 1302 Western Avenue 206/624–2187

TAYLOR SHELLFISH FARMS OYSTER BAR ($$)

www.tayloroysterbars.com

You'll find more than just oysters at this Pioneer Square raw bar, where all the shellfish comes from their own Puget Sound fishery.

E16 410 Occidental Avenue S 206/502–4060 Lunch and dinner daily

TRACE ($$)

www.traceseattle.com

International influences flavor the dishes here, served as small plates, large plates, sharing plates and tasting menus.

E15 1112 4th Avenue 206/264–6060 Breakfast and lunch Mon–Fri, brunch Sat–Sun, dinner Mon–Sat

WILD GINGER ($$)

The most popular and perhaps most lauded Asian restaurant in Seattle serving legendary Fragrant Duck, with a bar that's bulging with beautiful people.

D14 1401 3rd Avenue 206/623–4450 Dinner nightly

ZEITGEIST KUNST AND KAFFEE ($)

Fresh espresso, inviting ambience, art displays and internet access make this Pioneer Square café a popular haunt.

E17 171 S Jackson Street 206/583–0497 Daily 7–7

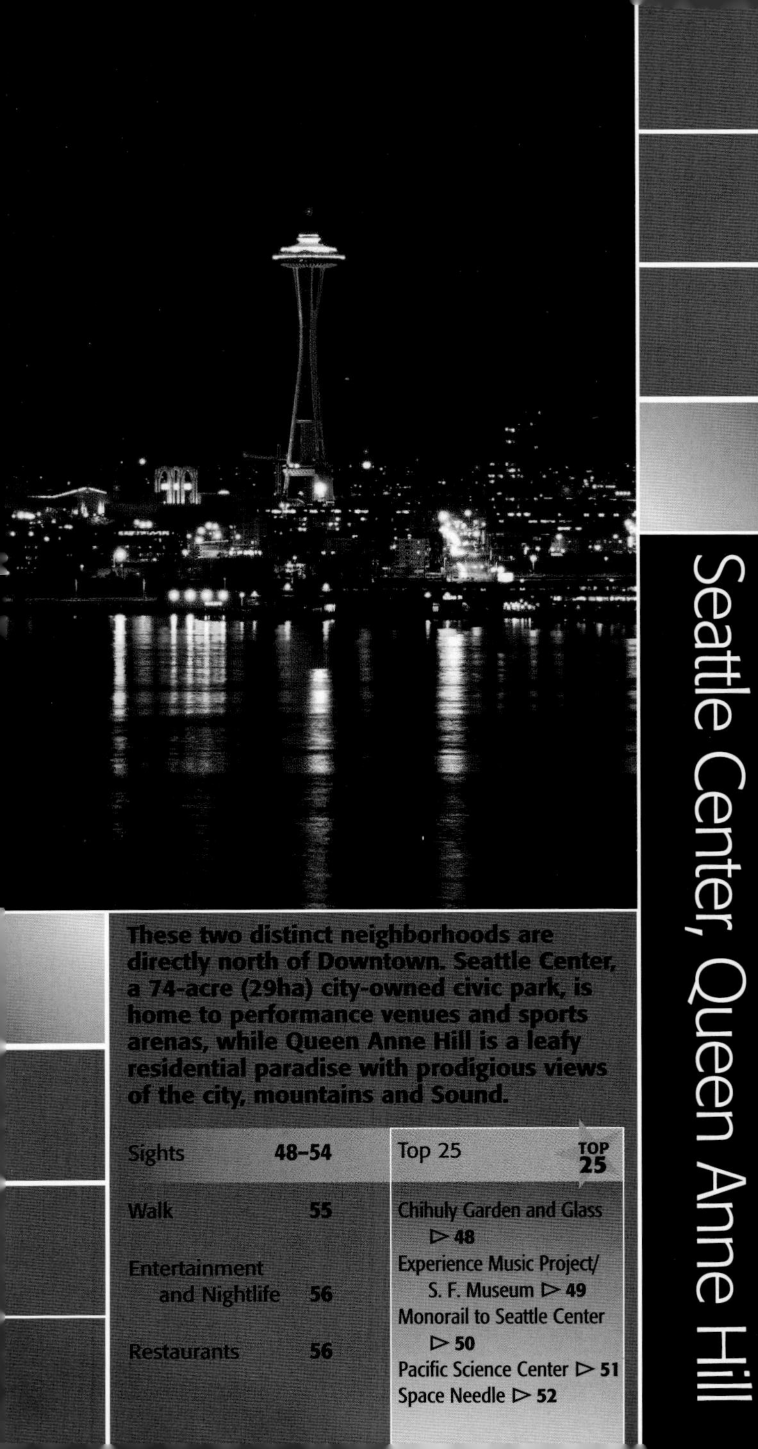

Seattle Center, Queen Anne Hill

These two distinct neighborhoods are directly north of Downtown. Seattle Center, a 74-acre (29ha) city-owned civic park, is home to performance venues and sports arenas, while Queen Anne Hill is a leafy residential paradise with prodigious views of the city, mountains and Sound.

Top 25 TOP 25

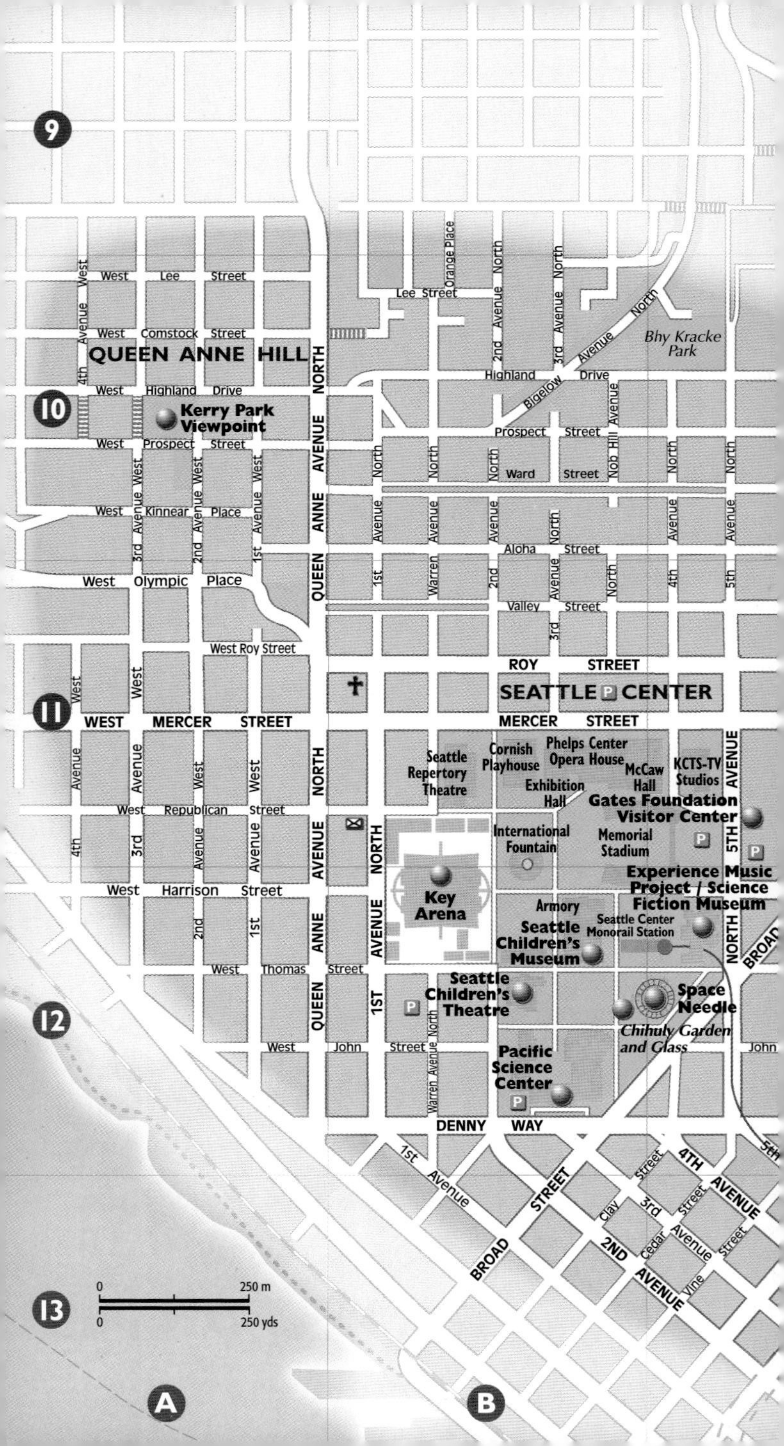

9
10
11
12
13
QUEEN ANNE HILL
Kerry Park Viewpoint
West Lee Street
West Comstock Street
West Highland Drive
West Prospect Street
West Kinnear Place
West Olympic Place
West Roy Street
WEST MERCER STREET
West Republican Street
West Harrison Street
West Thomas Street
West John Street
4th Avenue West
3rd Avenue West
2nd Avenue West
1st Avenue West
QUEEN ANNE AVENUE NORTH
1ST AVENUE NORTH
Warren Avenue North
Lee Street
Orange Place
2nd Avenue North
3rd Avenue North
Bigelow Avenue North
Bhy Kracke Park
Highland Drive
Prospect Street
Ward Street
Nob Hill Avenue North
Aloha Street
Valley Street
4th Avenue North
5th Avenue North
ROY STREET
SEATTLE CENTER
MERCER STREET
Seattle Repertory Theatre
Cornish Playhouse
Phelps Center
Opera House
McCaw Hall
KCTS-TV Studios
Exhibition Hall
Gates Foundation Visitor Center
International Fountain
Memorial Stadium
Key Arena
Experience Music Project / Science Fiction Museum
Armory
Seattle Center Monorail Station
Seattle Children's Museum
Seattle Children's Theatre
Space Needle
Chihuly Garden and Glass
Pacific Science Center
5TH AVENUE NORTH
BROAD
John
DENNY WAY
1st Avenue
BROAD STREET
2ND AVENUE
3rd Avenue
4TH AVENUE
Clay Street
Cedar Street
Vine Street
5th
0 250 m
0 250 yds
A
B

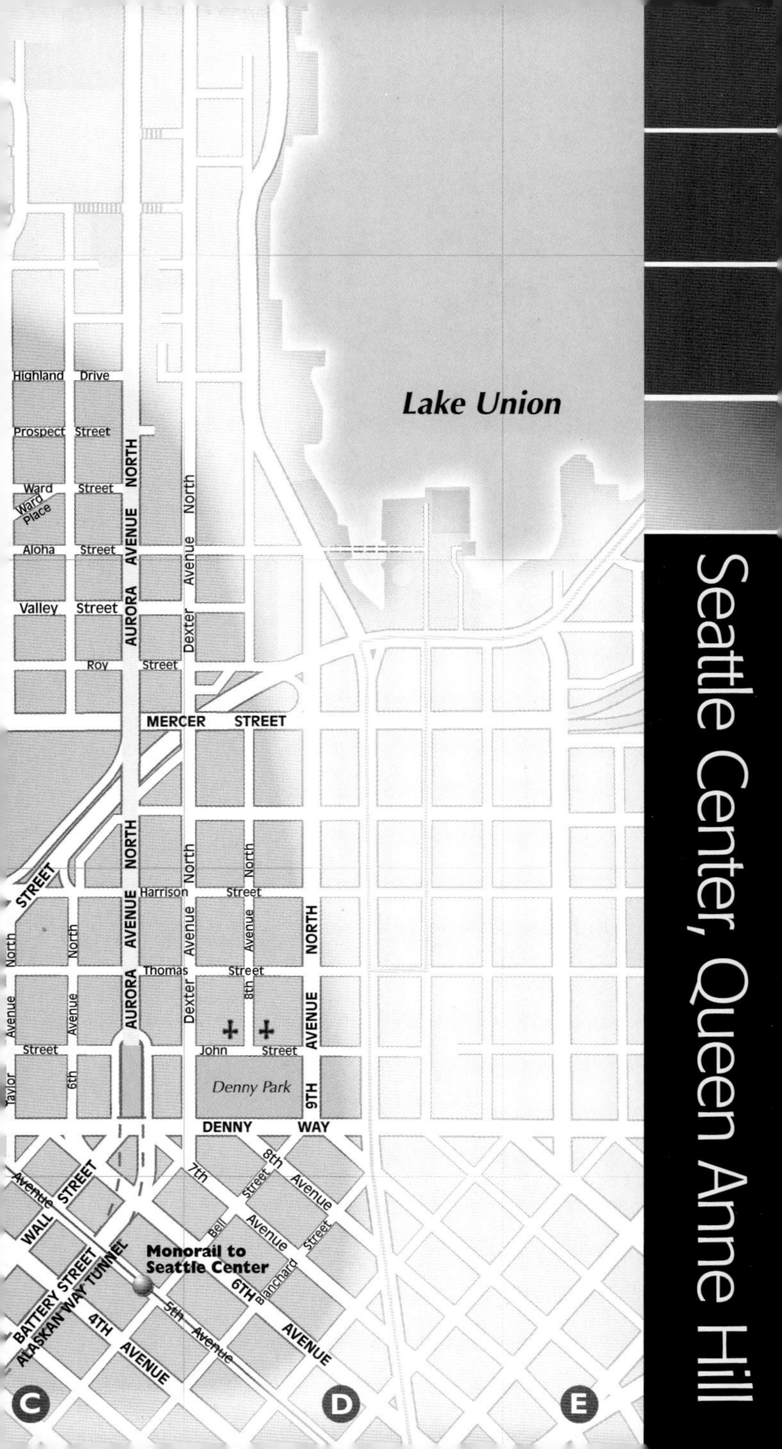
Seattle Center, Queen Anne Hill
Lake Union
Highland Drive
Prospect Street
Ward Street
Ward Place
Aloha Street
Valley Street
Roy Street
MERCER STREET
AURORA AVENUE NORTH
Dexter Avenue North
Harrison Street
Thomas Street
John Street
8th Avenue North
9TH AVENUE NORTH
Taylor Avenue North
6th Avenue North
STREET
Denny Park
DENNY WAY
WALL STREET
BATTERY STREET
ALASKAN WAY TUNNEL
Monorail to Seattle Center
4TH AVENUE
5th Avenue
6TH AVENUE
7th Avenue
8th Avenue
Bell Street
Blanchard Street
C
D
E

Chihuly Garden and Glass

TOP 25

Vibrant glass appears to be growing at the Chihuly gallery (left), in the shadow of the Space Needle (right)

THE BASICS

www.chihulygardenand glass.com
B12
305 Harrison Street at Seattle Center
206/753–4940
Mon–Thu 10–10, Fri–Sun 10am–11pm (last admission one hour before closing)
Collections Café
Monorail
Expensive

HIGHLIGHTS

- The Glasshouse
- *The Sun*
- *Glass Forest*
- *Persian Ceiling*

TIPS

- Time your visit so you can witness how the changing light transforms the outdoor exhibits as day turns into night.
- Children are allowed, but for peace of mind, you might want to leave them (and any clumsy adults) at home.

Tacoma-born Dale Chihuly is a world-renowned glass artist, and this extensive collection of his intricate and gloriously colorful works is displayed in a 1.5-acre (0.6ha) garden, a sparkling glasshouse and an eight-room exhibition hall.

The artist At the forefront of the development of glass as fine art, Dale Chihuly has examples of his work in countless important museums and public buildings around the world. After studying and then teaching at the Rhode Island School of Design, he worked at Venice's Venini glass factory. Back in his home state, he co-founded the Pilchuck Glass School, near Seattle, and has been showered with awards.

Garden and Glasshouse Some say you can't improve on nature, but this garden presents a compelling challenge to that belief, with colorful glass forms seemingly growing among the trees and flowers. The whole set piece is anchored by four stunning glass sculptures. The focal point is the Glasshouse, an arched structure housing a 100ft (33m) long floral sculpture of richly glowing reds, oranges and yellows.

Exhibition and theater Eight galleries make up the exhibition, which displays some of Chihuly's finest works and traces the development of his ideas and techniques. The darkened rooms show the artworks to their best advantage, their vibrant colors and organic shapes gleaming through the gloom.

The distinctive form of the Experience Music Project (left) holds a range of interactive exhibits (right)

TOP 25 Experience Music Project/ Science Fiction Museum

This futuristic gathering place is half rock museum and half science fiction shrine—a temple to American music and science fiction unrivaled in both style and daring.

Gift to the city Microsoft co-founder Paul Allen idolized Seattle-born Jimi Hendrix and imagined a space to exhibit his personal collection of Hendrix memorabilia. Over time, the vision expanded beyond Hendrix: The museum would grow to explore all of American popular music and science fiction literature and film through engaging interactive and interpretive exhibits.

The design Allen hired renowned architect Frank O. Gehry to create a structure that was as rebellious and free-spirited as rock 'n' roll itself. To jumpstart his creative thinking, Gehry cut up and rearranged several electric guitars. This process gave birth to the museum's bold colors, swooping curves and reflective metal surface.

Discover what's inside The museum is divided equally between rock 'n' roll and science fiction. The 85ft (26m) Sky Church features music film and video by day and live bands by night. Trace the development of the electric guitar or view objects of Seattle's grunge scene, jam on real instruments in the Sound Lab, or record your own voice. The Science Fiction Museum pays tribute to the biggest names of the genre by displaying movie props, first editions and interviews with sci-fi pioneers.

THE BASICS

www.empsfm.org
C12
325 5th Avenue North at Seattle Center
206/770–2700 or 877/367–7361
Late May–Aug daily 10–7; Sep–late May 10–5
3, 4, 16
Monorail
Good
Expensive

DID YOU KNOW?

- Jazz musician Les Paul pioneered electric guitar technology in Seattle by using a solid body. The Gibson company adopted the design and use it to this day.
- Jimi Hendrix was born in Seattle in 1942. In the late 1960s he revolutionized electric guitar playing with his radical fusion of jazz, rock, soul and blues.

Monorail to Seattle Center

TOP 25

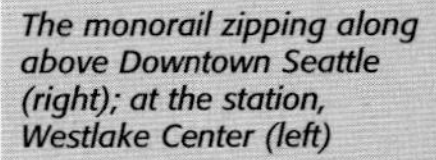
The monorail zipping along above Downtown Seattle (right); at the station, Westlake Center (left)

THE BASICS

www.seattlemonorail.com
www.seattlecenter.com
C13
Downtown station 3rd floor, Westlake Center; Seattle Center Station adjacent to EMP/sfm
Seattle Center 206/684–7200
Monorail daily every 10–15 min (▷ 118). Seattle Center grounds Mon–Fri 7.30am–11pm, Sat–Sun 8.30am–11pm
Armory/Center House; closed Thanksgiving, Christmas and New Year
3, 4
Inexpensive

Riding the Monorail to Seattle Center is like being in an old sci-fi movie. You buzz around the city like a giant insect and sweep past some of the city's major sights before alighting at the Center House.

World's Fair leftovers The Seattle Center district, like the monorail, is the legacy of the 1962 World's Fair. Once a Native American ceremonial ground, and later host to traveling circuses, the 74-acre (30ha) site didn't assume its present form until the fair. The monorail has now run continuously longer than any other monorail in the world.

Museum city Every day, this elevated train carries up to 7,000 passengers between Westlake Center, Seattle's retail core, and Seattle Center, its entertainment hub. There, you can take a trip in the Space Needle's glass elevator (▷ 52) or visit museums and galleries, including the Seattle Children's Museum (▷ 54), Experience Music Project/Science Fiction Museum (▷ 49), several craft galleries and the Pacific Science Center (▷ 51). Seattle Center is also home to opera, ballet, excellent theater companies and several professional sports teams. Also, Seattle's major festivals take place on the center grounds. Stop in the Center House for something to eat or try one of the restaurants close by.

Easy walking Stroll through the remarkable Chihuly Garden and Glass (▷ 48) and the nearby Peace Garden southwest of the Needle, or enjoy a picnic on the grass by the International Fountain.

The high arches of the Pacific Science Center (right); enjoying an interactive exhibit (left)

TOP 25 Pacific Science Center

As you approach the Pacific Science Center, you enter another world. Gothic arches and an inner courtyard of reflecting pools, platforms and footbridges indicate you are in for something special.

Sputnik's legacy In 1962, the American scientific community was still smarting from the Soviet Union's unexpected launch of the Sputnik spacecraft. Determined to restore confidence in American science and technology, US officials pulled out all the stops when they built the US Science Pavilion for the Seattle World's Fair. The building reopened after the fair ended as the Pacific Science Center.

Science made easy A visit here can happily fill half a day. The exhibits bring scientific principles to life and make learning fun. In an outdoor exhibit, Water Works, you can move a water cannon to activate whirligigs or attempt to move a 2-ton ball suspended on water. Children can ride a high-rail bike for a bird's-eye view. The Body Works exhibition lets you measure your stress level or grip strength or see what your face looks like with two left sides. Adventures in 3Dimensions shows how our brains process 3D imagery, and there are lots of robots—giant insects, dinosaurs and more—many of them interactive. Live animal exhibits include Insect Village and a Tropical Butterfly House. The Studio and the Portal to Current Research have regularly updated exhibits about new scientific and medical research. There's also a Planetarium and a live science stage.

THE BASICS

www.pacificsciencecenter.org
B12
200 2nd Avenue N (Seattle Center)
206/443-2001, 206/443-2844
Mon–Fri 10–5, Sat–Sun 10–6
Fountains Café
1, 2, 3, 4, 6, 8, 19, 24, 35
Monorail
Very good
Expensive; half-price with CityPass

DID YOU KNOW?

- The Center was designed by Minoru Yamasaki.
- ThePacific Science Center was the first museum in the United States to be founded as a science and technology center.

Space Needle

TOP 25

Almost everywhere you go in Seattle the Space Needle is there, towering over the city

THE BASICS

www.spaceneedle.com
C12
400 Broad Street at Seattle Center
Observation Deck daily 8am–midnight
SkyCity Restaurant
3, 4
Monorail
Wheelchair access
Expensive; half-price with CityPass; free with dinner at restaurant

DID YOU KNOW?

- The Space Needle sways about 1in (3cm) for every 10mph (16kph) of wind.
- The Needle experienced an earthquake of 6.8 on the Richter scale (in 2001), and is equipped to withstand jolts up to 9.2.

The Space Needle's height and futuristic design have made it Seattle's most well-known landmark. From the observation deck the view is stunning on a clear day.

The city's symbol The 605ft (184m) Space Needle was built in 1962 for Seattle's futuristic World's Fair. Rising 200ft (61m) above Seattle's highest hill, the structure is visible over a wide area. The steel structure weighs 3,700 tons and is anchored into the foundations with 72 huge bolts, each 32ft (10m) long by 4in (10cm) in diameter. The structure is designed to withstand winds up to 150mph (242kph). If you ride in the glass-walled elevator to the top during a snowstorm, it appears to be snowing upward.

Observation deck Each year, more than a million visitors ride one of the three glass elevators to the observation deck at the 520ft (159m) level. Informative displays point out more than 60 sites around the area and recount Space Needle trivia. Screens linked to rooftop cameras allow for a closer view. A reservation at the SkyCity Restaurant, at the 500ft (152m) level, gets you to the observation deck free of charge. The restaurant rotates one complete turn every 47 minutes, giving a 360-degree panorama during your meal.

Tall and strong There are 848 steps between the bottom of the basement and the top of the Observation Deck. When the Space Needle was built in 1962, it was the tallest building west of the Mississippi River.

More to See

GATES FOUNDATION VISITOR CENTER

www.gatesfoundation.org

With a mission to help poor people worldwide make better lives for themselves, Bill and Melinda Gates set up a foundation that has distributed grants totaling more than $30 billion. This inspiring visitor center has displays and videos showing how the foundation works.

C11 440 5th Avenue N 206/709-3100, ext 7100 Tue–Sat 10–5 (to 6 early June–late Aug) Free Monorail

KERRY PARK VIEWPOINT

This tiny park on Queen Anne Hill has a great view of Downtown and features Doris Chase's steel sculpture *Changing Form*.

A10 W Highland Drive and 2nd W 2

KEY ARENA

www.keyarena.com

The arena is home to many sports teams, including the Seattle Storm and Seattle University Redhawks basketball teams, and the Rat City Rollergirls. It also hosts big-name stadium concerts and shows such as Disney on Ice.

B12 Seattle Center 206/684-7200 1, 2, 3, 4, 24 to Seattle Center Monorail

SEATTLE CHILDREN'S MUSEUM

www.thechildrensmuseum.org

A magical world where children can shop for groceries in a child-size market, visit an African village or create enormous soap bubbles.

B12 The Armory/Center House, first level, 305 Harrison Street, Seattle Center 206/441-1768 Mon–Fri 10–5, Sat–Sun 10–6 3, 4, 16, 24 to Seattle Center Monorail

SEATTLE CHILDREN'S THEATRE

www.sct.org

Recognized worldwide for its innovative programing, SCT is a prized cultural resource for families.

B12 201 St. Thomas Street, Seattle Center 206/441-3322 Performances Sep to mid-May Fri–Sun 1, 2, 3, 4, 16 to Seattle Center Monorail

The nighttime view of the city from Kerry Park, seen through the sculpture

Lovely Streets of Queen Anne

From the hipster hot spot of Queen Anne to the peaceful neighborhoods of the upper hill, taking in marvelous views of Seattle's skyline.

DISTANCE: 4 miles (6.25km) **ALLOW:** 2.25 hours

START

EASY STREET RECORDS

B11 1, 2, 13

1 Start at Easy Street Records, one of Seattles iconic independent music stores, on the corner of Mercer Street and 1st Avenue N. The shop hosts performances by touring bands weekly.

2 Leave the shop and walk east on Mercer for three blocks. Turn right and enter the Seattle Center campus between the Pacific Northwest Ballet and the Intiman Theater (▷ 56).

3 Walk straight and you'll see the International Fountain, a favorite spot on warm days. Southeast lies Armory/Center House and its food court.

4 Walk west along the southern edge of Key Arena (▷ 54). Continue west to Queen Anne Avenue N. Turn right, go north to Roy Street, then take a soft left turn up the hill on West Queen Anne Drive.

5 Continue on this street onto 1st Avenue W. There's an imposing hill for a few blocks, but the views are fine.

6 Turn left on W Highland Drive. Walk two blocks to Kerry Park for views of Mount Rainier and the Space Needle (▷ 52–53). Continue west on W Highland Drive.

7 Veer to the right onto 8th Avenue W until it meets 7th Avenue W, and then go north on 7th to West McGraw Street. Turn right here, grab a coffee and a pastry at the Macrina Bakery, and continue on for seven blocks to Queen Anne Avenue N.

8 Stroll south along Queen Anne Avenue N, which is lined with shops, restaurants and bars. Stop for a beverage at the Hilltop Ale House.

END

HILLTOP ALE HOUSE

A8 2, 3, 4, 13, 45, 82

Entertainment and Nightlife

INTIMAN THEATER

www.intiman.org

Pulitzer Prize-winning regional company that focuses on modern plays and the classics. The season runs May through December.

B11 201 Mercer Street, Seattle Center 206/441–7178 1, 2, 13

ON THE BOARDS/ CENTER FOR CONTEMPORARY PERFORMANCE

Presentations integrate dance, theater, music and visual media.

A11 100 W Roy Street 206/217–9888 15, 18

PACIFIC NORTHWEST BALLET

Renowned company under the direction of former New York City Ballet dancers. The repertory mixes contemporary and classical, plus rarely performed Balanchine ballets.

B11 Phelps Center, 301 Mercer Street, Seattle Center 206/441–9411 1, 2, 13

SEATTLE OPERA

One of the preeminent opera companies, with four or five productions September through May.

B11 McCaw Hall, 321 Mercer Street, Seattle Center 206/389–7676 1, 2, 13

SEATTLE REPERTORY THEATER

Seattle's oldest theater company presents updated classics, recent off-Broadway and new works. October–May.

B11 Bagley Wright Theater, Seattle Center 206/443–2222 1, 2, 13, 15, 18

WORLD SPORTS GRILLE

An upscale sports bar with TV screens, billiard tables and gourmet food bar, it also retains the original bar from New York's Algonquin Hotel.

D11 731 Westlake N 206/223–0300 Mon–Fri until 2am

Restaurants

PRICES

Prices are approximate, based on a 3-course meal for one person.

$$$ over $50
$$ $30–$50
$ under $30

5 SPOT ($)

www.chowfoods.com

An ever-changing menu that concentrates on different regions every few months: You never know if you'll get Creole catfish or New England clam chowder.

A9 1502 Queen Anne Avenue N 206/285–7768 Breakfast, lunch and dinner daily

CROW ($$)

www.eatatcrow.com

This airy Lower Queen Anne bistro has wowed diners since opening in 2004. An open kitchen complements the industrial aesthetic

C10 823 5th Avenue N 206/283–8800 Dinner daily

MALENA'S TACO SHOP ($)

In a gorgeous neighborhood at the apex of Queen Anne Hill, this diminutive taco shop serves great tortillas, burritos, tamales and more.

Off map 620 W McGraw Street 206/284–0304 Lunch and dinner Tue–Sun; closed Mon

SKYCITY AT THE NEEDLE ($$$)

At 500ft (152m) above Seattle, the pricey dinners are only average, but the view is priceless.

C12 400 Broad Street (in the Space Needle) 206/905–2173 Lunch and dinner daily, brunch on weekends

Capitol Hill to Washington Park

Two very different areas: Capitol Hill is a left-leaning district known for its gay community, vintage theaters and trend-setting bistros. Washington Park, on the other hand, features lavish homes, expansive parks and lakefront beaches.

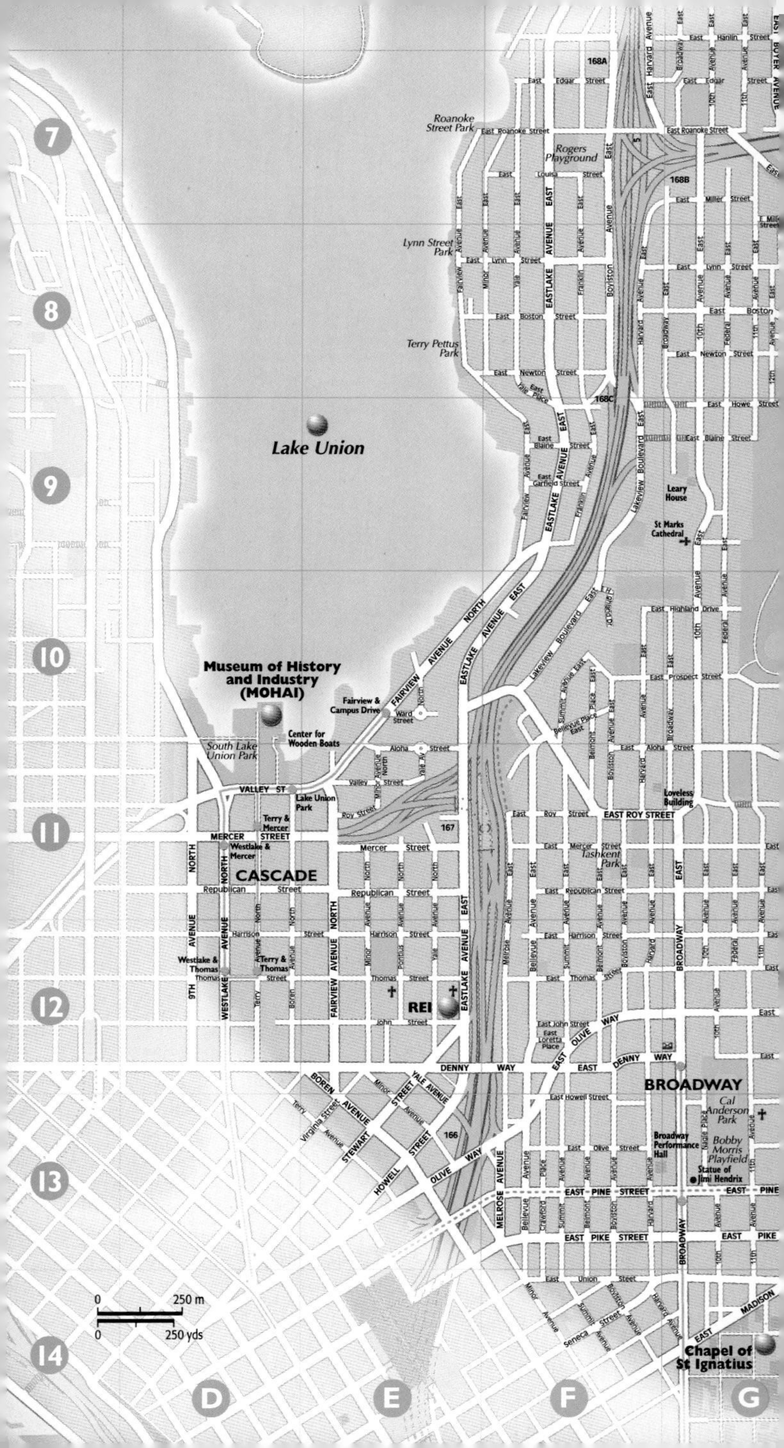

Lake Union
Museum of History and Industry (MOHAI)
Center for Wooden Boats
South Lake Union Park
Lake Union Park
Fairview & Campus Drive
Terry & Mercer
Westlake & Mercer
Westlake & Thomas
Terry & Thomas
CASCADE
REI
Roanoke Street Park
Rogers Playground
Lynn Street Park
Terry Pettus Park
Leary House
St Marks Cathedral
Loveless Building
Tashkent Park
BROADWAY
Cal Anderson Park
Bobby Morris Playfield
Broadway Performance Hall
Statue of Jimi Hendrix
Chapel of St Ignatius
EASTLAKE AVENUE
FAIRVIEW AVENUE NORTH
WESTLAKE AVENUE NORTH
9TH AVENUE NORTH
MERCER STREET
VALLEY ST
DENNY WAY
OLIVE WAY
EAST ROY STREET
EAST PINE STREET
EAST PIKE STREET
EAST MADISON
MELROSE AVENUE
BOREN AVENUE
STEWART STREET
HOWELL STREET
YALE AVENUE
Lakeview Boulevard East
168A
168B
168C
167
166
0
250 m
250 yds
7
8
9
10
11
12
13
14
D
E
F
G

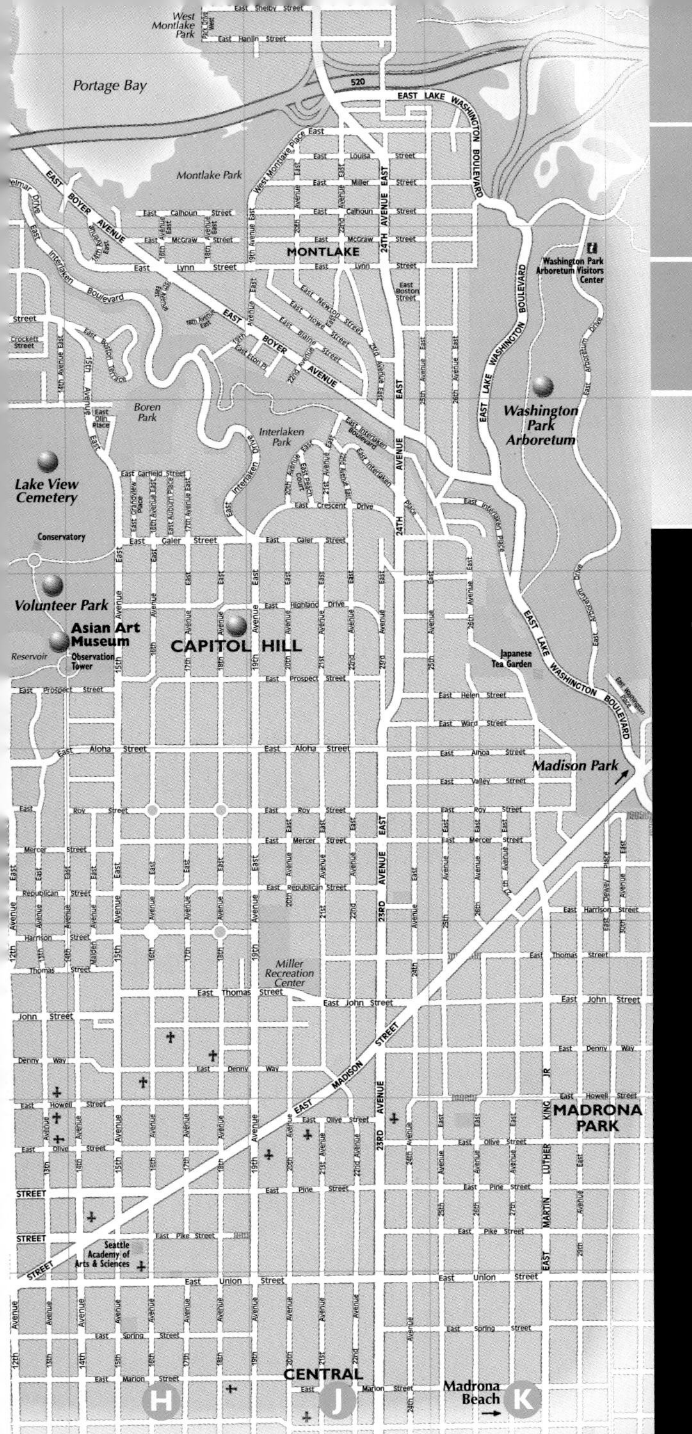
Portage Bay
West Montlake Park
520
Montlake Park
MONTLAKE
EAST LAKE WASHINGTON BOULEVARD
EAST BOYER AVENUE
24TH AVENUE EAST
Washington Park Arboretum Visitors Center
Washington Park Arboretum
Boren Park
Interlaken Park
Lake View Cemetery
Conservatory
Volunteer Park
Asian Art Museum
Reservoir
Observation Tower
CAPITOL HILL
Japanese Tea Garden
Madison Park
Miller Recreation Center
23RD AVENUE
EAST MADISON STREET
MADRONA PARK
MARTIN LUTHER KING JR
Seattle Academy of Arts & Sciences
CENTRAL
Madrona Beach
H
J
K

Capitol Hill

HIGHLIGHTS

- Volunteer Park (▷ 67) and its 1912 conservatory
- Sipping cappuccino at an authentic coffeehouse
- Dancing into the wee hours at Neighbours nightclub
- Shopping for vintage clothing on Broadway
- Dining at a romantic bistro

TIP

- Walk to the Hill from Downtown—it's less than a 20-minute stroll, and parking can be nightmarish.

It's not quite the Haight-Ashbury, but this neighborhood is the undisputed center of Seattle's counterculture. It's a delightful mélange of urban parks, authentic coffeehouses, trendy bistros and stylish bars.

A street scene The stretch of Broadway between Roy Street (at the north end) and Madison Street (at the south end) pulses with activity at all hours of day and night. Street performers, teen punk-rockers and colorful personalities can be found throughout the mile-long corridor, but there are two epicenters of activity—the intersection of Broadway and John Street, and the intersection of Broadway and Pike Street.

Taverns, bars and clubs The Hill, as it's affectionately known, is rapidly becoming a

Drop in for coffee (top left) or lie back and relax at a massage shop (top middle) after a hard day's sightseeing in the Capitol Hill district; the annual Gay Pride Parade takes place through Capitol Hill (bottom left); a statue on Broadway celebrates one of the city's most famous sons, Jimi Hendrix (right)

destination nightspot. Party seekers come from miles around—often from across Lake Washington—to drink, dance and revel in the area's seemingly endless array of dive bars, upscale lounges and pulsating dance clubs. (The Pike/Pine corridor alone is loaded with bars and clubs, both gay and straight.)

Breathing space For fresh air and open spaces, head for Cal Anderson Park, one of the nation's loveliest public parks. It was originally called Lincoln Park and centered on the Lincoln Reservoir, but in 2000 the water was put underground and a subsequent remodeling of the park endowed its more than 7 acres (nearly 3ha) with new water features, sports and play areas, walking and bicycling paths and open spaces. It's named for Washington's first openly gay congressman, who died in 1995.

THE BASICS

G12, H10

10, 11, 12, 43, 49

Lake Union

TOP 25

Life by the water (left) and kayaking (right) on Lake Union; Route 99 bridge (far right)

THE BASICS

E9
70, 71, 72, 73 on Fairview/Eastlake
South Lake Union Streetcar from Westlake
Argosy Tours (▷ 119); Lake Union Houseboat & Canal Tour (☎ 206/355–0133), Seattle Seaplanes (▷ 119)

DID YOU KNOW?

- Seattle has more houseboats than anywhere east of Asia, and most are on Lake Union.
- Lake Union took its name from a pioneer's speech in which he dreamed that one day a lake would form "the union" between Puget Sound and Lake Washington.
- Visitors who want to experience lakefront living can stay in a "bunk and breakfast" anchored here
- Gas Works Park, on the north side, offers great views of Downtown.

In a neighborhood shared by tugboats and research ships, ducks and racoons, Lake Union's houseboaters swap dry land and backyards for a vibrant lifestyle on this bustling lake.

Floating world The houseboat life started more than a century ago on Lake Union. A sawmill that opened on the lake in 1881 attracted a community of loggers and their hangers-on. Many of these woodsmen built makeshift shelters by tying felled logs together and erecting tarpaper shacks on top. Before long, thousands of shacks floated on the waterways. These "floating homes," Seattle's earliest houseboats, were a far cry from the gentrified versions made familiar by the film *Sleepless in Seattle*.

Boats and stores Today Lake Union is a lively mix of marine activity, houseboat living and expensive dining and shopping. Start your visit with a stroll, passing the Center for Wooden Boats on the south end, to get right into the seafaring spirit. Then, for a true Lake Union experience, go out on the lake. You can rent sailboats, skiffs or kayaks, and explore on your own, or sign on with a tour. Back ashore, there are the numerous good restaurants on Chandler's Cove.

Seaplane central The Lake is also a bustling aquatic airport; Kenmore Air, the world's largest seaplane airline, operates numerous flights to and from Lake Union daily. Sight-seeing flights are available too.

KISW

REI

TOP 25

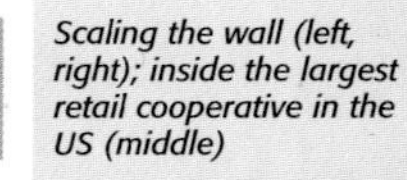

Scaling the wall (left, right); inside the largest retail cooperative in the US (middle)

THE BASICS

www.rei.com
E12
222 Yale Avenue N
206/223-1944
Mon–Sat 9–9, Sun 10–7
World Wrapps on-site
70, 25, 66
South Lake Union Streetcar to Westlake & Mercer
Good
Pinnacle climbing; equipment repair and rentals

DID YOU KNOW?

- REI is the largest retail cooperative in the United States, with more than 1.4 million members.
- The REI building was constructed with materials that are either recycled or have minimal impact on the environment, and the company has invested in renewable energy for its stores.
- The Seattle store's 65ft (20m) climbing pinnacle is the world's highest.

The popularity of Recreational Equipment Inc., Seattle's premier retailer of outdoor wear and equipment, is legendary. The annual garage sale draws hordes of devotees, who gather like pilgrims at a holy shrine.

It began with an ice axe REI had humble origins in the 1930s. It was founded by Seattle climbers Lloyd and Mary Anderson, when Lloyd's search for a high-quality, affordable ice axe ended in frustration—the one he wanted was not sold in the United States but could be ordered only from Europe. Anderson purchased one and soon his climbing buddies wanted their own. In 1938, 23 climbers banded together to form a member-owned cooperative in order to obtain mountaineering equipment unavailable in the United States.

Try it out REI's flagship store is the place to try before you buy. Under staff guidance, you can, for example, don a harness and scale the store's free-standing 65ft (20m) high indoor pinnacle. There is a "hiking trail," where you can test the toughness of boots; a trail designed for mountain-bike test rides; and test stations for camp stoves and water filtration systems. REI also carries a large selection of outdoor apparel and books.

Big business In 2013, REI posted worldwide sales of more than $2 billion. Not bad for a cooperative. REI now has 129 stores in 25 US states; it averages six to eight new store openings each year.

Blossom-covered shrubs adorn the water's edge of the Japanese Garden

TOP 25

Washington Park Arboretum

This large botanical collection owes its origins to Edmond S. Meany, founder of the University of Washington's School of Forestry. Today's garden combines exotics with virtually every woodland plant indigenous to the area.

Green oasis Meany initiated a seed exchange with universities around the world. As a result, you can walk through a variety of ecological zones and enjoy a rich diversity of flora.

The Japanese Garden On the west side of Lake Washington Boulevard, tucked away behind a wooden fence, lies the restful Japanese Garden. The garden was designed in 1960 by Juki Lida, a Tokyo landscape architect, who personally supervised both its planning and construction. Elements of the garden—plants, trees, water, rocks—and their placement represent a miniature world of mountain, forest, lake, river and tableland. There's also a ceremonial teahouse.

Waterfront Trail This 1.5-mile (2km) trail, originating behind the Museum of History and Industry (▷ 67), winds through marshland on floating platforms and footbridges. At Foster Island it cuts under the new road bridge and continues through what was once a Native American burial ground to Duck Pond. To experience this convergence of man and nature from the water, rent a canoe from the waterfront Activity Center and go for a paddle through water lilies among the mallards.

THE BASICS

www.depts.washington.edu/wpa
www.seattle.gov/parks/parkspaces/japanese-garden
off map at J7
Between E Madison Street and Hwy 520, and 26th Avenue E and Arboretum Drive E (Graham Visitor Center at 2300 Arboretum Drive E)
206/543-8800; Japanese Garden 206/684-4725
Daily dawn–dusk; Japanese Garden Mar–Sep daily; Oct–Feb Tue–Sun
11 None
Waterfront and woodland trails free; Japanese Garden inexpensive

DID YOU KNOW?

- The Arboretum covers an area of 230 acres (93ha).
- Botanist Edmond S. Meany test-planted imported seeds in his own garden, and later transplanted the plants on campus.

More to See

ASIAN ART MUSEUM

www.seattleartmuseum.org

AAM's Volunteer Park galleries showcase the museum's permanent collection, numbering more than 7,000 objects, from China, Japan, Korea, India and Southeast Asia. The extensive Chinese collection, dating from the neolithic period through the 19th century, includes ancient burial ceramics, ritual bronzes, snuff bottles and the wonderful *Monk Caught at the Moment of Enlightenment*. Japanese galleries feature Buddhist sculpture, metalwork, textiles, ink painting and calligraphy. AAM also offers Sunday afternoon concerts.

G10 1400 E Prospect Street 206/654-3100 Wed–Sun 10–5 (Thu till 9); open some holiday Mons Fair Moderate; free 1st Thu of month and 2nd Thu 5–9 pm; free for seniors 1st Fri of month; free for families 1st Sat of month 10

CHAPEL OF ST. IGNATIUS

www.seattleu.edu/chapel/

This sublime chapel is Seattle University's architectural gift to the city. Architect Steven Holl visualized the structure as "seven bottles of light in a stone box," with light bouncing off the tinted baffles to create a halo effect on the surrounding walls.

G14 901 12th Avenue, near Marion Street on Capitol Hill 206/296-6075 Mon–Thu 7am–10pm, Fri 7–7, Sat 8–5, Sun 8–10. Regular liturgies 2, 12

LAKE VIEW CEMETERY

www.lakeviewcemeteryassociation.com

Seattle's pioneers are buried here, but it's the graves of martial arts cult star Bruce Lee (near the top of the hill) and his son, Brandon, that draw visitors.

G9 1554 15th Avenue E at E Garfield, Capitol Hill 10

MADISON PARK

In this neighborhood beach park, on the western shore of Lake Washington, you can sunbathe on the grassy slope. There's also a bathhouse and a swimming dock with a diving board. Lifeguards operate throughout the summer.

Inside the lofty main hall at the Museum of History and Industry (left)

The Museum of History and Industry occupies a historic building on South Lake Union (below)

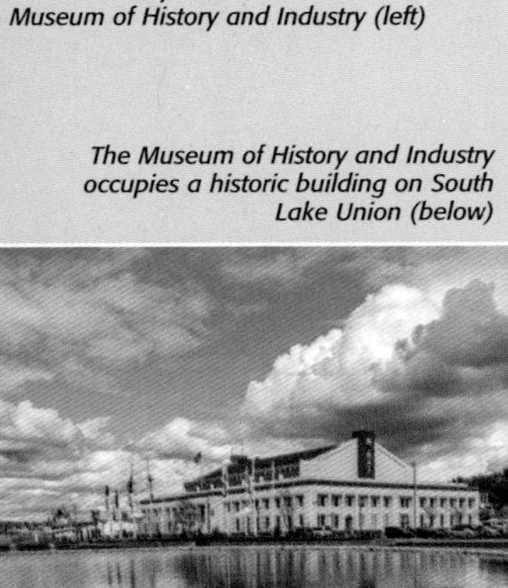

Off map (▷ 98) The foot of E Madison Street at 43rd Avenue E 11 206/322-1582 Daily dawn–dusk

MUSEUM OF HISTORY AND INDUSTRY (MOHAI)

www.seattlehistory.org

In 2012, after a 10-year conversion of a former armory on South Lake Union, MOHAI moved into its new, larger home. With more space to display its iconic items from Seattle's past and to regularly add new history-in-the-making exhibits, it's a lively and engaging place. The Bezos Center for Innovation reflects the range of items and ideas generated in the local area, including information about some of the latest projects. Maritime Seattle explores the city's relationship with the sea, including a working periscope to view the city. Perhaps the most engaging exhibit of all is True Northwest: The Seattle Journey, which traces the settlement and development of the area through a series of set-piece displays, each combining artifacts and images of a particular era with interactive devices. Temporary exhibitions explore particular aspects of the city in greater detail; recent offerings have included stories from Jewish merchants of the past, and the history of chocolate (with tastings).

D10 860 Terry Avenue N 206/324-1126 Daily 10–5 (to 8 Thu) South Lake Union Streetcar from Westlake Center Park Excellent Moderate, free 1st Thu of month

VOLUNTEER PARK

Volunteer Park was named during the Spanish-American War of 1898 to honor those who had served as soldiers. The park offers more than a lush green space. There's a water tower to climb for 360-degree views, the Asian Art Museum (▷ 66), or take a stroll through the conservatory to admire the thousands of plants that simulate botanical environments from around the world.

G10 Between E Galer and E Prospect and 15th and 11th avenues Park daily 6–10. Conservatory Tue–Sun 10–4 10, 12

Black Sun *(Isamu Noguchi, 1969), a sculpture in Volunteer Park*

A Walk in Washington Park Arboretum

Visit Seattle's woodsy urban paradise and walk through a wetland trail, viewing the city's flora and fauna in its natural habitat.

DISTANCE: 4.25 miles (7km) **ALLOW:** 2.5 hours

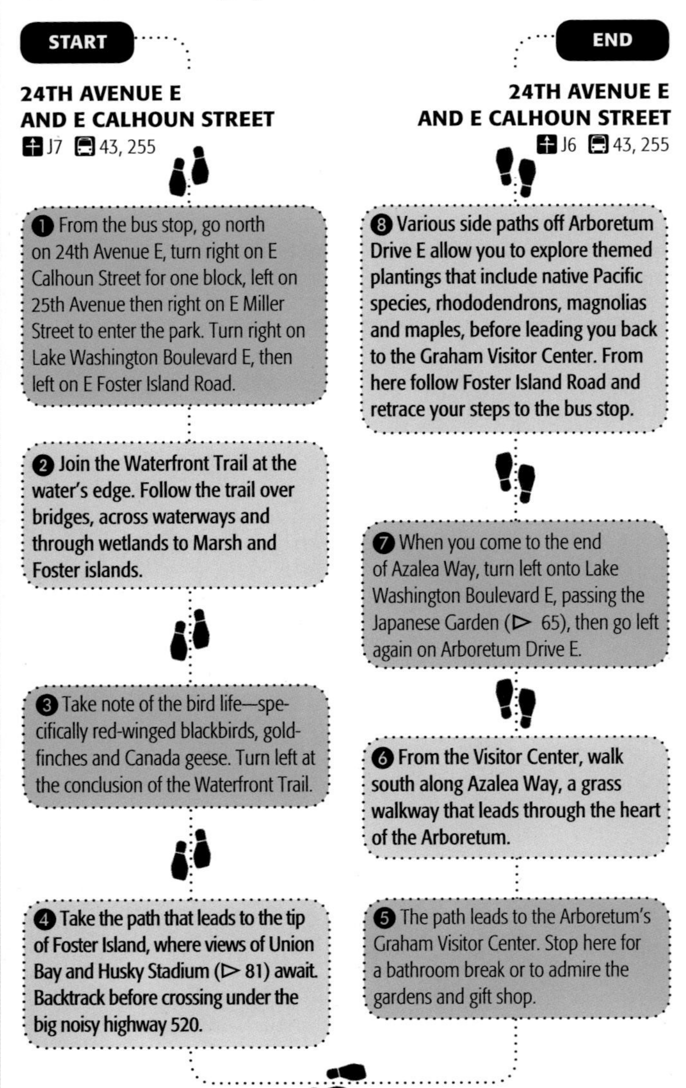

START

24TH AVENUE E AND E CALHOUN STREET

J7 43, 255

1 From the bus stop, go north on 24th Avenue E, turn right on E Calhoun Street for one block, left on 25th Avenue then right on E Miller Street to enter the park. Turn right on Lake Washington Boulevard E, then left on E Foster Island Road.

2 Join the Waterfront Trail at the water's edge. Follow the trail over bridges, across waterways and through wetlands to Marsh and Foster islands.

3 Take note of the bird life—specifically red-winged blackbirds, goldfinches and Canada geese. Turn left at the conclusion of the Waterfront Trail.

4 Take the path that leads to the tip of Foster Island, where views of Union Bay and Husky Stadium (▷ 81) await. Backtrack before crossing under the big noisy highway 520.

5 The path leads to the Arboretum's Graham Visitor Center. Stop here for a bathroom break or to admire the gardens and gift shop.

6 From the Visitor Center, walk south along Azalea Way, a grass walkway that leads through the heart of the Arboretum.

7 When you come to the end of Azalea Way, turn left onto Lake Washington Boulevard E, passing the Japanese Garden (▷ 65), then go left again on Arboretum Drive E.

8 Various side paths off Arboretum Drive E allow you to explore themed plantings that include native Pacific species, rhododendrons, magnolias and maples, before leading you back to the Graham Visitor Center. From here follow Foster Island Road and retrace your steps to the bus stop.

END

24TH AVENUE E AND E CALHOUN STREET

J6 43, 255

Shopping

EDIE'S SHOES

www.ediesshoes.com
Fashion and comfort in the same shoe? You can have it here, with footwear for all, plus great bags.
F13 319 E Pine Street
206/839-1111
Mon–Sat 10–7, Sun 12–5

ELLIOTT BAY BOOK COMPANY

www.elliottbaybook.com
More than 150,000 titles grace the bookshelves here, and the store also hosts author readings and other events.
G13 1521 10th Avenue 206/624-6600 or 800/962-5311
Mon–Thu 10–10, Fri–Sat 10am–11pm, Sun 10–9

GHOST GALLERY

www.ghostgalleryart.com
Paintings and prints by established and emerging Seattle artists.
F12 504 Denny Way, through fence by Hillcrest Market Mon, Wed–Fri 11–7, Sat–Sun 11–6

LE FROCK

www.lefrockonline.com
Recycled and vintage clothing for men and women, and designer samples.
F13 613 E Pike Street 206/623-5339 Mon–Sat 10–7, Sun 12–6

SONIC BOOM RECORDS

An adorable independent music shop with the latest releases in all styles.
H11 514 15th Avenue E 206/568-2666
Mon–Sat 10–10, Sun 10–7

TWICE-SOLD TALES

www.twice-sold-tales.biz
Wonderful secondhand bookstore.
G12 1833 Harvard Avenue 206/324-2421
Mon– Thu 10–9, Fri–Sat 10am–11.30pm, Sun 11–8

URBAN OUTFITTERS

www.urbanoutfitters.com
New and vintage clothing; also housewares, jewelry and gifts.
G12 401 Broadway E
206/322-1800 Wed 10–9, Thu–Sat 10–10, Sun 10–8

Entertainment and Nightlife

HARVARD EXIT THEATRE

www.landmarktheatres.com
Consistently strong program featuring off-beat current releases in an old Capitol Hill Mansion.
F11 807 E Roy Street
206/323-0587

RICHARD HUGO HOUSE

www.hugohouse.org
Welcoming literary arts gathering place. Frequent readings and other events.
G13 1634 11th Avenue 206/322-7030

ROCK BOX

www.rockboxseattle.com
Enjoy upscale karaoke, with only your chosen party looking on, in one of the private rooms at this Japanese-style venue.
G13 1603 Nagle Place
206/302-7625 Mon–Wed 4pm–2am, Thu 4pm–3am, Fri–Sat 3pm–4am, Sun 3pm–2am

FILM

Seattle is a great place for film buffs. The city hosts an annual International Film Festival in May and June that is the largest in the United States. Other festivals include Women in Cinema and Jewish, Irish and Asian festivals.

SUN LIQUOR LOUNGE

www.sunliquor.com
A welcoming and unpretentious little cocktail bar serving superior classics made with liquor from their own distillery and fresh-squeezed juices.
F13 607 Summit Avenue 206/860-1130

Restaurants

PRICES

Prices are approximate, based on a 3-course meal for one person.
$$$ over $50
$$ $30–$50
$ under $30

ARAYA'S PLACE ($)
www.arayasplace.com
Vegan Thai food is served buffet-style at lunch and from the extensive menu at dinner.
K11 2808 E Madison Street 206/402-6634
Lunch and dinner daily

ALTURA ($$$)
www.alturarestaurant.com
The daily-changing menu of artistically presented Italian dishes is likely to include seasonal wild ingredients alongside local heirloom ingredients.
G11 617 Broadway E
206/402-6749
Dinner Tue–Sat

CAFÉ PRESSE ($)
www.cafepresseseattle.com
European-inspired coffee and cuisine. Full bar with excellent cocktails; televised international soccer on weekends.
G14 1117 12th Avenue 206/709-7674
Breakfast, lunch and dinner daily

CAFFÈ LADRO ($)
www.caffeladro.com
Adirondack chairs line the front of this friendly neighborhood coffee shop.
A11 15th Avenue E on N Capitol Hill
206/267-0551

ESPRESSO VIVACE ($)
www.espressovivace.com
The best place to get a cup of coffee in the city, with umbrella-shaded tables; perfect for people-watching.
G12 532 Broadway Avenue 206/325-7186
Lunch and dinner daily

LARK ($$)
www.larkseattle.com
With a small-plate menu featuring charcuterie, local vegetables and everything in between, this bistro has a devoted following.
G14 926 12th Avenue
206/323-5275
Dinner Tue–Sun

PINE BOX ($)
www.pineboxbar.com
With a commitment to local, ethically produced ingredients (and craft beers), this pub serves good soups, salads, sandwiches and pizzas.
F13 1600 Melrose Avenue 206/588-0375
Dinner daily, brunch Sat–Sun

ESPRESSO

In a city known for excellent coffee, there is no better neighborhood for java sipping than Capitol Hill. Some of the best coffee hot spots in Seattle are Espresso Vivace (▷ this page) and Downtown's Bauhaus (▷ 42).

QUEEN BEE CAFÉ ($)
www.queenbeecafe.com
The delicious soups, salads and home-baked crumpets are enough to entice you in; the fact that all its profits go to local charities is a bonus.
J12 2200 E Madison Street, Suite B 206/757-6314 Daily 7–7

RESTAURANT MARRON ($$)
www.restaurantmarron.com
Co-owned by the chef, this chic restaurant serves modern French cuisine.
F11 806 E Roy Street
206/322-0409
Dinner Wed–Sun

SERAFINA ($$)
www.serafinaseattle.com
Rustic Italian cuisine by candle-light and an outdoor deck for summer.
F8 2043 Eastlake Avenue E 206/323-0807
Lunch Mon–Fri, dinner nightly

TANGO TAPAS RESTAURANT & LOUNGE ($$)
www.tangorestaurant.com
Stylish dining on the edge of Capitol Hill.
F13 1100 Pike Street
206/583-0382
Dinner nightly

TAQUERIA GUAYMAS ($)
www.tacosguaymas.com
Authentic and delicious Mexican food.
G13 1519 Broadway E
206/860-3871 Lunch and dinner daily

University District

The U-District is a delightful *mélange* of residential streets, urban avenues and roomy campus quadrangles. Its best-known attraction is University Way, a vibrant boulevard lined with boutiques, record shops and ethnic restaurants.

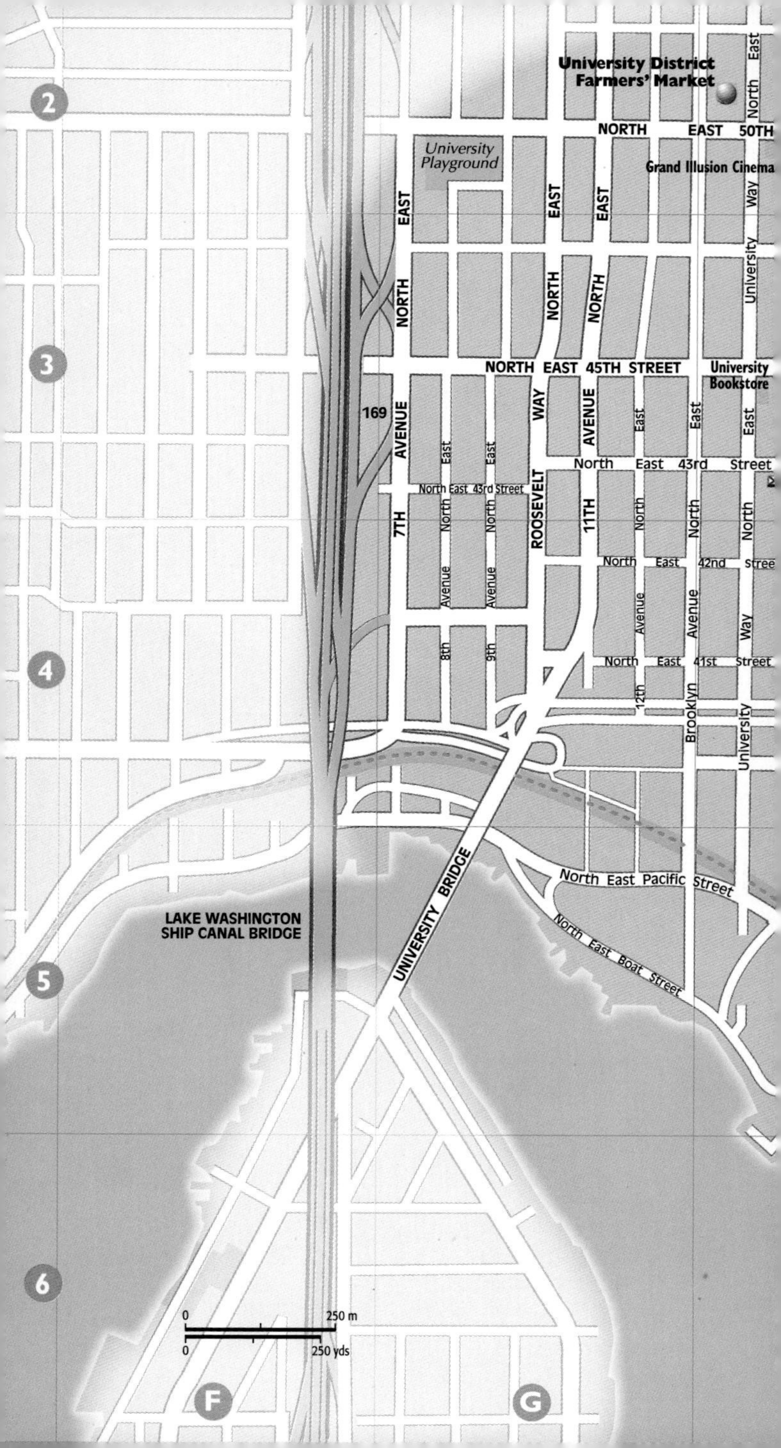

University District Farmers' Market
University Playground
Grand Illusion Cinema
NORTH EAST 50TH
NORTH EAST 45TH STREET
University Bookstore
169
7TH AVENUE NORTH EAST
ROOSEVELT WAY NORTH EAST
11TH AVENUE NORTH EAST
North East 43rd Street
8th Avenue North East
9th Avenue North East
12th Avenue North East
Brooklyn Avenue North East
University Way North East
North East 42nd Street
North East 41st Street
UNIVERSITY BRIDGE
North East Pacific Street
North East Boat Street
LAKE WASHINGTON SHIP CANAL BRIDGE
0
250 m
250 yds
2
3
4
5
6
F
G

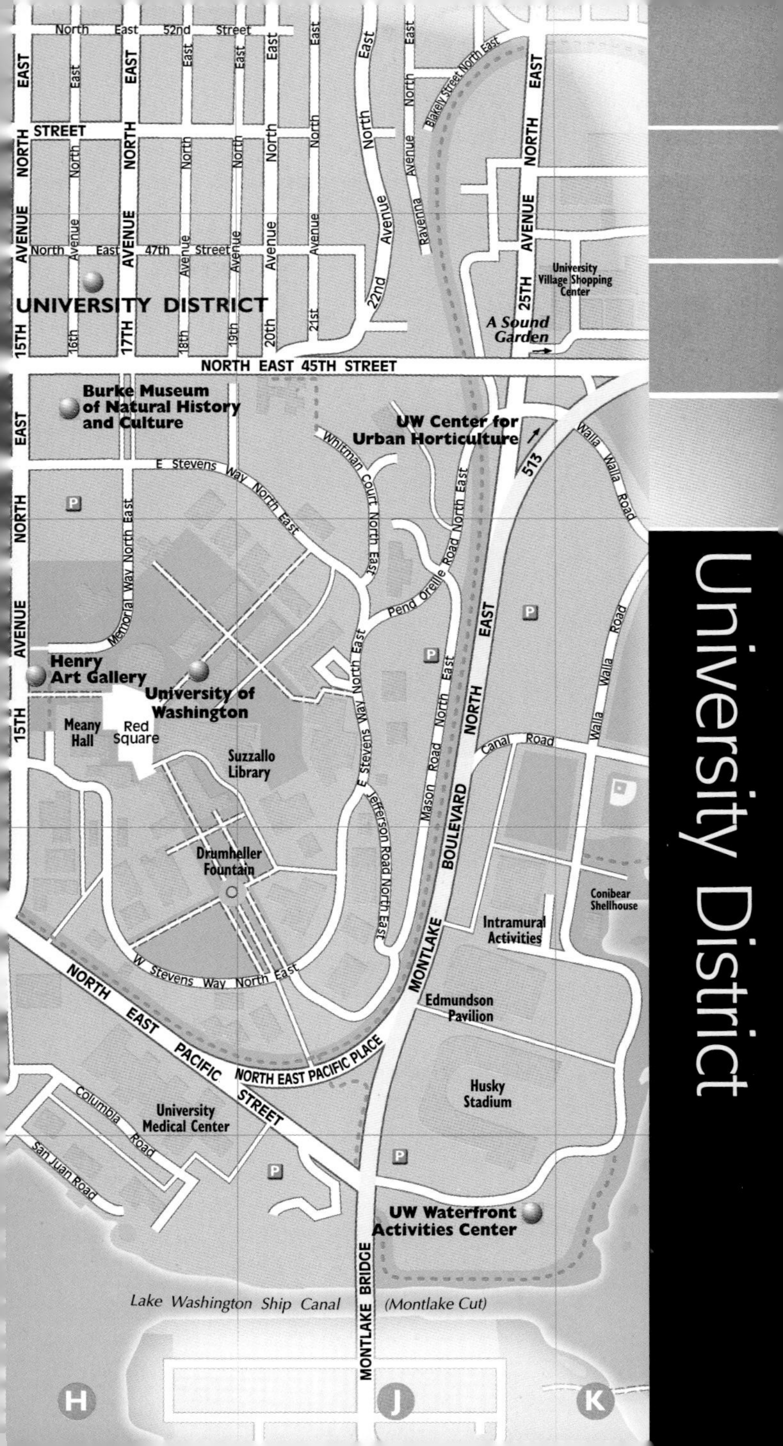

University District
UNIVERSITY DISTRICT
North East 52nd Street
North East 47th Street
NORTH EAST 45TH STREET
15TH AVENUE NORTH EAST
16th Avenue North East
17TH AVENUE NORTH EAST
18th Avenue North East
19th Avenue North East
20th Avenue North East
21st Avenue North East
22nd Avenue North East
Ravenna Avenue North East
Blakely Street North East
25TH AVENUE NORTH EAST
University Village Shopping Center
A Sound Garden
Burke Museum of Natural History and Culture
UW Center for Urban Horticulture
Whitman Court North East
E Stevens Way North East
Memorial Way North East
Pend Oreille Road North East
Walla Walla Road
513
Henry Art Gallery
University of Washington
Meany Hall
Red Square
Suzzallo Library
Mason Road North East
Jefferson Road North East
MONTLAKE BOULEVARD NORTH EAST
Canal Road
Drumheller Fountain
Conibear Shellhouse
Intramural Activities
W Stevens Way North East
Edmundson Pavilion
NORTH EAST PACIFIC STREET
NORTH EAST PACIFIC PLACE
Husky Stadium
Columbia Road
San Juan Road
University Medical Center
UW Waterfront Activities Center
Lake Washington Ship Canal
(Montlake Cut)
MONTLAKE BRIDGE
P
H
J
K

Burke Museum of Natural History and Culture TOP 25

DID YOU KNOW?

- The museum's anthropological division has the largest Northwest Coast collection of Indian objects in the western United States.
- The 65,000 bird specimens in the ornithology collection account for 95 percent of North American species.
- Before the Burke opened, a number of ethnic groups came to the museum for private "blessing" ceremonies to consecrate their installations.

The Burke's permanent collection demonstrates at once a keen artistic sense, genuine respect for the cultural traditions of featured groups and a scientist's attention to detail.

The Burke's beginnings The museum's origins date back to 1879, when four enthusiastic teenagers calling themselves the Young Naturalists set about collecting Northwest plant and animal specimens, a popular hobby at the time. Their collection grew, so much that to house it a museum was built on the University of Washington campus in 1885. Over the next 20 years, the number of specimens increased, and today they form the basis of the Burke's vast collection. A project is underway to provide a new building for the museum, expected to open by 2019.

With its origins dating back to 1879, the Burke Museum has amassed a huge collection of more than 15 million objects, including the skeletal remains of a dinosaur (left, bottom middle); children are fascinated by the Bug Blast Exhibition (top right) and love to examine the old bones (bottom right)

Treasures on display As you walk through the entrance, a stunning glass display case demands immediate attention. It highlights selected treasures from this vast collection, and gives you an idea of what's in store. In the halls beyond, two exhibits showcase the museum's strong suits: natural history and ethnography. The Pacific Voices exhibit conveys the variety of Pacific Rim cultures, from New Zealand to the northwest coast of Canada. By framing the exhibit around the celebrations and rituals that are central to each culture, museum objects are placed within their appropriate context. Constructed "sets," photo murals, sounds and informative text communicate the importance of cultural traditions. The Life and Times of Washington State exhibit is a chronological journey through 545 million years of Washington history.

THE BASICS

www.burkemuseum.org
H3
University of Washington campus at NE 45th Street and 17th Avenue NE
206/543–5590
Daily 10–5 (1st Thu of month until 8)
Burke Café
43, 68, 70, 71, 72, 73
Very good
Moderate. "Dollar Deal"—pay an extra dollar for same-day admission to the Henry Art Gallery

Henry Art Gallery

TOP 25

The renowned Skyspace *exhibit (left); a cool, contemporary gallery houses the collection (right)*

THE BASICS

www.henryart.org
H4
UW campus at 1400 15th Avenue NE and NE 41st Street
206/543–2280 or 206/543–2281 (scheduled tours/events)
Wed–Sun 11–4 (Thu, Fri until 8)
Molly's Café
25, 43, 70, 71, 72, 73
Very good
Moderate; free Thu

HIGHLIGHTS

- The Monsen Collection of Photography
- Regular artists' lectures, symposia and film showings

DID YOU KNOW?

- Founded in 1927, the Henry was the first public art museum in the state.

The Henry Art Gallery, dedicated to contemporary art, collects and encourages artists to produce thought-provoking works, and invites visitors to discover the power of their innovative imagery.

The gallery The art museum of the University of Washington has 14,000sq ft (1,302sq m) of gallery space and includes an auditorium, education studio and sculpture court, with the elliptical *Skyspace* by the artist James Turrell.

Skyspace, *Light Reign* The piece is the first installation of its kind to combine two key aspects of Turrell's work: skyspace and exterior architectural illumination. It provides both a meditative gallery experience and a public art component that can be viewed from outside the museum.

The collection A cornerstone of the collection is the Monsen Collection of Photography, from vintage prints to contemporary explorations of the medium. The permanent collection also includes 19th- to 20th-century landscape painting, modern art by Stuart Davis, Robert Motherwell and Lionel Feininger, and the international Costume and Textile Collection, exhibited on a rotating basis.

Learn as you go In addition to films, lectures and tours, the museum presents discussions of a current exhibition and outlines how an exhibition is developed.

The University campus entrance (left); students gather on the steps bordering Red Square (right)

TOP 25

University of Washington

The University campus was originally planned as a fairground for Seattle's 1909 Exposition celebrating the Alaska Gold Rush. Much of the design, including Rainier Vista, has been preserved.

Vistas and fountains To begin your tour stop at the visitor information center to pick up a free self-guided tour map and an events schedule. As you walk, you'll see buildings in a variety of architectural styles, from turreted Denny Hall to cathedral-like Suzzallo & Allen Library. The Suzzallo & Allen faces Red Square, a student gathering place. Only the Broken *Obelisk* sculpture and three campanile towers break the horizontal line of this plaza, which is bordered by Meany Hall, a performing arts venue.

Elsewhere To the west lies the Henry Art Gallery (▷ 76). To the north, the old campus quadrangle is especially inviting in late March, when rows of pink Japanese cherry trees burst into bloom. Continuing toward the university's north entrance, you come to the Burke Museum (▷ 74–75) and UW's observatory (▷ 81). Head toward the Waterfront Activities building (▷ 78) to rent a canoe.

The Ave One block west of the campus lies University Avenue (University Way), known as "the Ave." Here, a multitude of ethnic restaurants, music and bookstores and second-hand stores share the avenue with kids who call the neighborhood "home."

THE BASICS

www.washington.edu

H4

Between 15th and 25th avenues, NE and Campus Parkway and NE 45th Street; (UW Visitor Center, 4014 University Way NE at Campus Parkway)

206/543–9198

Mon–Fri 8–5

25, 43, 70, 71, 72, 73

Good

DID YOU KNOW?

- The university moved to its present location in 1891.
- Most locals call the university "U Dub."
- Suzzallo & Allen Library was modeled after King's College Chapel in Cambridge, England.
- Husky Stadium has seats for 72,000 people.

TIP

- Rent a canoe or rowboat at the University's Waterfront Activities Center; you can paddle across the Montlake Cut to the Washington Park Arboretum (▷ 65).

More to See

A SOUND GARDEN

One of Seattle's small treasures. Doug Hollis's ingenious work consists of 12 steel towers supporting wind-activated organ pipes that create gentle sounds on windy days. Restricted access and photo ID required; gates open weekdays 9–5; no access on weekends.

Off map at J3 Behind NOAA building, 7600 Sand Point Way NE 74, 75

UNIVERSITY DISTRICT

This area includes the University of Washington (▷ 77), "the Ave," and University Village, a complex of tasteful specialty stores, markets and cafés. "The Ave" is full of ethnic restaurants and interesting shops.

H3 Many including 7, 43, 70, 71

UNIVERSITY DISTRICT FARMERS' MARKET

www.seattlefarmersmarkets.org

Farmers and artisans from across western Washington bring their produce and crafts to this popular Saturday morning market.

H2 University Way NE and NE 50th Street 70, 71, 72, 73, 74

UW CENTER FOR URBAN HORTICULTURE

Founded in 1984, the center includes a variety of garden areas and a 74-acre (30ha) wildlife habitat. Principal attractions include a herbarium and the Union Bay Natural Area, a waterfront open space excellent for bird-watching.

Off map at J3 3501 NE 41st Street 206/543-8616 Daily dawn–dusk 25, 65, 75

UW WATERFRONT ACTIVITIES CENTER

www.washington.edu/ima/wac

The center sits on the shore of the Montlake Cut, where canoes and rowboats are available for rental in summer to explore the twisting, calm-water channels of the nearby Washington Park Arboretum.

J6 On Union Bay, behind Husky Stadium 206/543-9433 Center: daily 25, 43, 65, 67, 68

University District Farmers' Market (above)

Waterfront Activities Center (right)

Through Campus and Beyond

Stroll through UW's picturesque campus and visit a host of renowned University-affiliated institutions.

DISTANCE: 2.5 miles (6.25km) **ALLOW:** 1.5 hours

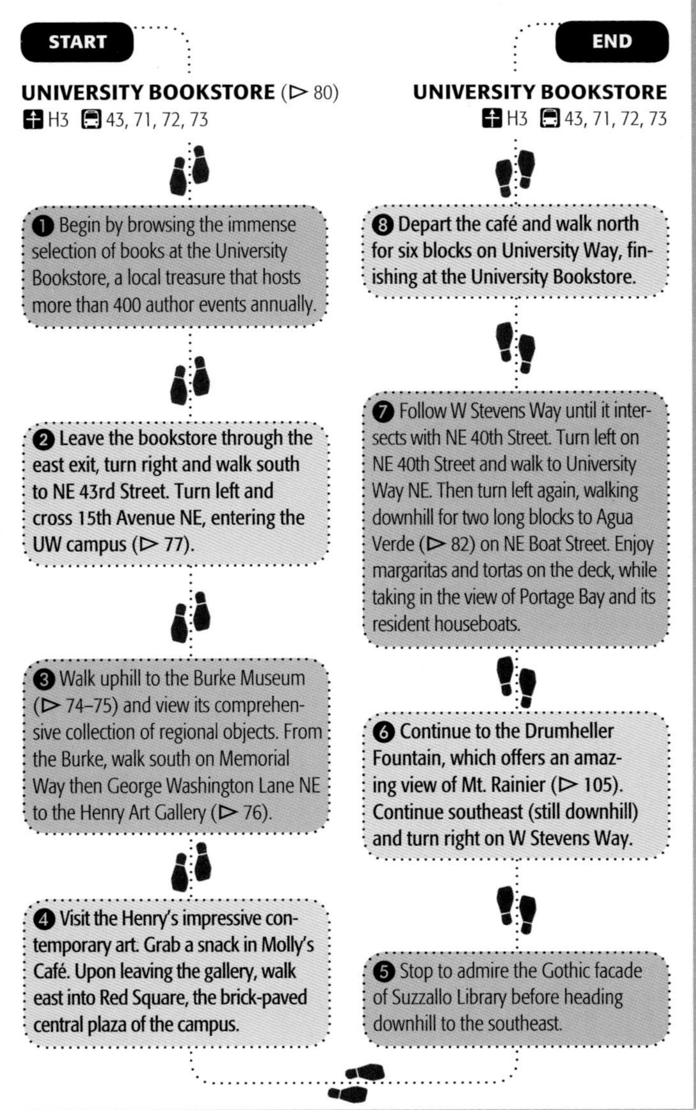

START

UNIVERSITY BOOKSTORE (▷ 80)
H3 43, 71, 72, 73

❶ Begin by browsing the immense selection of books at the University Bookstore, a local treasure that hosts more than 400 author events annually.

❷ Leave the bookstore through the east exit, turn right and walk south to NE 43rd Street. Turn left and cross 15th Avenue NE, entering the UW campus (▷ 77).

❸ Walk uphill to the Burke Museum (▷ 74–75) and view its comprehensive collection of regional objects. From the Burke, walk south on Memorial Way then George Washington Lane NE to the Henry Art Gallery (▷ 76).

❹ Visit the Henry's impressive contemporary art. Grab a snack in Molly's Café. Upon leaving the gallery, walk east into Red Square, the brick-paved central plaza of the campus.

❺ Stop to admire the Gothic facade of Suzzallo Library before heading downhill to the southeast.

❻ Continue to the Drumheller Fountain, which offers an amazing view of Mt. Rainier (▷ 105). Continue southeast (still downhill) and turn right on W Stevens Way.

❼ Follow W Stevens Way until it intersects with NE 40th Street. Turn left on NE 40th Street and walk to University Way NE. Then turn left again, walking downhill for two long blocks to Agua Verde (▷ 82) on NE Boat Street. Enjoy margaritas and tortas on the deck, while taking in the view of Portage Bay and its resident houseboats.

❽ Depart the café and walk north for six blocks on University Way, finishing at the University Bookstore.

END

UNIVERSITY BOOKSTORE
H3 43, 71, 72, 73

Shopping

ARTIST & CRAFTSMAN SUPPLY

www.artistcraftsman.com
Catering to all levels of creative types, this store has good quality art and craft supplies.
G3 4350 8th Avenue NE 206/545–0091 or 877/545–0091 Mon–Sat 9–7.30, Sun 10–6 72, 73

BRYN WALKER

www.brynwalker.com
Comfy, casual clothes for women, made of natural fibers, reign at this fun boutique.
Off map Corner of NE 45th Street and 25th Avenue NE 206/525–0698 Mon–Sat 9.30–9, Sun 11–6

BUFFALO EXCHANGE

www.buffaloexchange.com/location-details/seattle
This popular University District consignment store carries all manner of clothes, accessories, shoes and wigs.
H3 4530 University Way NE 206/545–0175 Mon–Sat 10–9, Sun 11–8 43, 71, 72, 73

BULLDOG NEWS

www.bulldognews.com
A newsstand on steroids, this neighborhood hangout has all the latest arts, lifestyle, business and sports publications. The on-site espresso bar is also excellent.
H3 4208 University Way NE 206/632–6397 Mon–Fri 6.30am–8pm, Sat–Sun 8–8 43, 71, 72, 73, 74

CALDWELL'S

www.caldwellsonline.com
Wonderful imports like folk art, textiles and jewelry from Central and South America, Africa and Asia.
Off map 2610 University Village NE 206/522–7531 Mon–Sat 9.30–9, Sun 11–6 25

KIRSTEN GALLERY

www.kirstengallery.com
Fine art—including marine art—prints, sculptures and ceramics represent the work of more than 40 artists. You can also spend a little quiet time in their beautiful zen garden.
Off map 5320 Roosevelt Way NE 206/522–2011 Wed–Sun 11–5 72, 73

MOKSHA CLOTHING & ACCESSORIES

An interesting range of mostly women's clothing includes local designers and vintage items.
H3 4542 University Way NE 206/632–2622 Mon–Thu 11–7, Fri–Sat 11–8, Sun 12–6 72, 73

INDEPENDENT SELLERS

Seattle has a number of excellent independent booksellers who are committed to bringing quality literature to the public, both blockbusters and smaller works appealing to a more specialized audience. But with the arrival of national chains and their well-appointed superstores, independents are feeling the pinch.

UNIVERSITY BOOKSTORE

www.seattleubookstore.com
One of the nation's largest university bookstores. Also sells art and office supplies, gifts and CDs.
H3 4326 University Way NE 206/634–3400 Mon–Fri 9–8, Sat 10–7, Sun 12–5 43, 71, 72, 73

UNIVERSITY VILLAGE

U-Village includes branches of a number of major players in the retail market.
Off map NE 45th Street and 25th Avenue NE, east of the campus 206/523–0622 Mon–Fri 8.30–5, Sat 9.30–9, Sun 11–6

VEGAN HAVEN

www.veganhaven.org
Nothing in this store has even come close to an animal, including vegan snacks and cookbooks, non-leather belts and wallets, cosmetics and dietary supplements.
Off map 5270 B University Way NE, corner of 55th 206/523–9060 Daily 10–8 72, 73

WOOLY MAMMOTH

This shoe store features a wide array of stylish kicks, including styles by Dankso, Chaco and more. Don't miss its sister shop, Five Doors Up, also along University Way.
H3 4303 University Way NE 206/632–3254 Mon–Fri 10–7, Sat 10–6, Sun 12–6 43, 71, 72, 73, 74

Entertainment and Nightlife

COLLEGE INN PUB
A bustling basement pub that has served college students for decades. The roaring hearth, pool tables and dart boards lend some flavor to the pub's lively atmosphere.
H4 4006 University Way NE 206/634–2307
43, 71, 72, 73, 74

GIGGLES
A University District haunt that attracts a college crowd. Microbrews on tap, cheap eats and hit-and-miss comedy. Thursdays and Sundays are open mic comic showcase nights.
G2 5220 Roosevelt Way NE 206/526–5653
66

GUILD 45TH
These two neighboring theaters are in the Wallingford district.
E3 2115 N 45th Street
206/547–2127

HUSKY STADIUM
The University of Washington's Huskies play PAC-10 football in fall at the Husky Stadium. Games are on Saturday.
J5 Montlake Boulevard NE 206/543–2200

INTERNATIONAL CHAMBER MUSIC SERIES
Renowned chamber music ensembles are performed from fall to spring as part of the University of Washington's "World Series at Meany Hall."
H4 Meany Theater, University of Washington, 4001 University Way NE
206/543–4880

JET CITY IMPROV
www.jetcityimprov.org
Three fast-paced improvised comedy shows, including the Twisted Flicks live movie redubbing show on the first weekend of the month.
Off map 5510 University Way NE
206/352–8291 Shows Thu–Fri at 8, Sat at 8 and 10.30 71, 72, 73

LITTLE RED HEN
A genuine country-and-western bar in the Green Lake neighborhood. Live country music, line dancing, karaoke, beer and snacks. Hunker down for an early-morning breakfast of chicken-fried steak.
Off map 7115 Woodlawn Avenue NE
206/522–1168
Daily 9am–2am

BIKE SHARE

Seattle's first bike share operation was launched in October 2014, introducing 500 bright green bicycles to the city streets. With docking stations in the University District, Downtown, Capitol Hill and South Lake Union, it's run by Pronto (www.prontocycleshare.com), and one-day and three-day passes are available, as well as helmets, which are compulsory wear. Download a copy of the Seattle Bike Map before you travel, www.seattle.gov/transportation/bikemaps.htm.

MEANY HALL'S WORLD DANCE SERIES
This October–May series features ballet, modern and ethnic dance; Seattle native Mark Morris is a frequent presence.
H4 Meany Hall, University of Washington
206/543–4880

OLYMPIC MUSIC FESTIVAL
www.olympicmusicfestival.org
Celebrated chamber musicians perform in an old barn on the Olympic Peninsula near Port Townsend, on weekends from June to September.
Off map 360/732–4800

SEVEN GABLES
This welcoming, converted residence in the University District features arthouse films.
G2 911 NE 50th Street
206/632–8820

UNIVERSITY OF WASHINGTON OBSERVATORY
Perfect for star-gazers. During bad weather you can watch a slide show on astronomy.
H3 Entrance to campus at NE 45th Street and 17th Avenue NE 206/543–2100
Apr–Sep. 1st and 3rd Wed of each month Free

Restaurants

PRICES

Prices are approximate, based on a 3-course meal for one person.

$$$	over $50
$$	$30–$50
$	under $30

AGUA VERDE ($)
www.aguaverde.com
An intimate Mexican-inspired cantina that's on the shore of Portage Bay. Great food, good views and a kayak rental shop downstairs make this a favorite of students.
H5 1303 NE Boat Street 206/545-8570
Lunch and dinner daily

CAFÉ LAGO ($$)
Rustic Italian café in Montlake, a short walk from the UW campus. A romantic atmosphere and incredible pizzas are the hallmarks of this favorite.
J8 2305 24th Avenue E
206/329-8005
Dinner nightly

DIE BIERSTUBE ($)
www.diebierstube.com
An authentic German tavern serving German beers and foods that include bratwurst and *landjäger*.
G2 6106 Roosevelt Way NE 206/527-7019
Dinner nightly

FLOWERS ($)
Funky, laid-back college bar with a vegetarian lunch buffet.
H3 4247 University Way NE 206/633-1903
Lunch and dinner daily

JAK'S GRILL ($$)
www.jaksgrill.com
Prime, dry-aged steaks, fine Washington wines and a full bar at this standout grill. A favorite post-game destination for well-off Husky fans.
Off map 3701 NE 45th Street 206/985-8545
Lunch Tue–Fri, dinner nightly

PAGLIACCI PIZZA ($)
Distinctive pizza, with traditional and offbeat toppings. Also at 426 Broadway E and 550 Queen Anne Avenue N.
H3 4529 University Way NE 206/726-1717

PAIR ($)
With a menu of exquisite small plates (including cassoulet Toulouse and smoked salmon toasts), this pint-size bistro makes a great spot for a romantic dinner.
Off map 5501 30th Avenue NE 206/526-7655
Dinner Tue–Sat

DIVERSE CUISINE

The University District is well-known for its diverse cuisine. Diners can choose between $7 noodle shops on "the Ave" and $40 prime steaks at outlying chop houses around the University. Thanks to the preponderance of college students, bar food is big here. But so is Asian, Italian and American fare. Whatever your choice of establishment, be prepared to share the restaurant with die-hard Husky fans.

PORTAGE BAY CAFÉ ($$)
www.portagebaycafe.com
With a menu featuring Dungeness crab, eggs benedict and smoked omelets with tomatoes and spinach, it's no surprise that this is one of the city's most popular breakfast locations.
G4 4130 Roosevelt Way NE 206/547-8230
Breakfast and lunch daily

SHULTZY'S SAUSAGE ($)
This modest, University District eatery features their signature sausages, made from high-quality ingredients, plus a rotating menu of beers. Other menu items include veggie burgers and a chicken sandwich. Shultzy's has a loyal following, whose photos decorate the walls.
H4 4114 University Way NE 206/548-9461
Lunch and dinner daily

TILTH ($$)
www.tilthrestaurant.com
Romantic eatery that keeps things local and organic. The cuisine is drop-dead delicious.
D3 1411 45th Street N 206/633-0801 Tue–Sun; brunch on weekends

Fremont, Ballard, Discovery Park

Once Seattle's bohemian hub, Fremont has evolved into an upscale version of its former self. Ballard, too, has morphed from a fisherman's outpost to a hipster's paradise. But through all of this change, Discovery Park remains the city's largest green space.

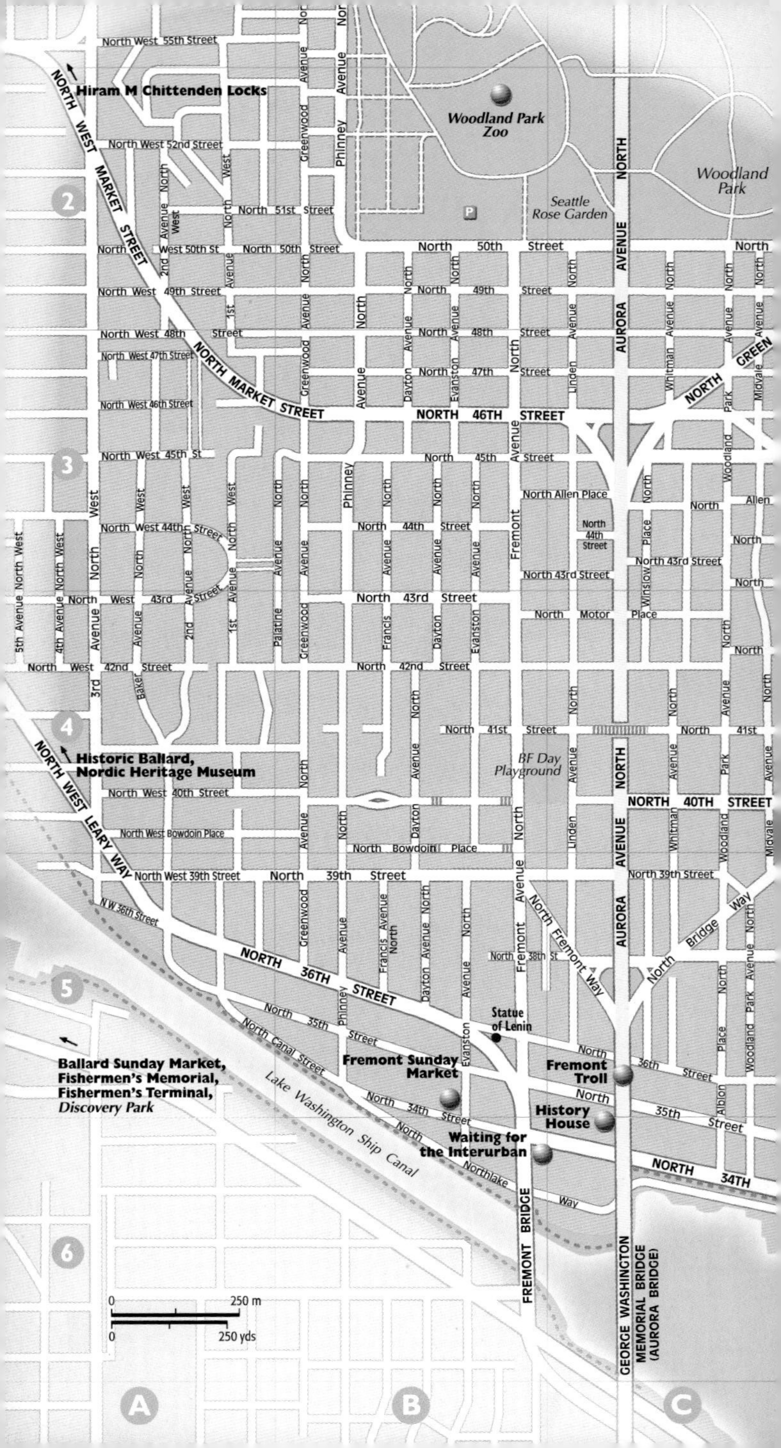

Hiram M Chittenden Locks
Woodland Park Zoo
Woodland Park
Seattle Rose Garden
North West 55th Street
North West 52nd Street
North West Market Street
North Market Street
North 46th Street
North 50th Street
North 49th Street
North 48th Street
North 47th Street
North 45th Street
North Allen Place
North 44th Street
North 43rd Street
North Motor Place
North 42nd Street
North 41st Street
North 40th Street
North Bowdoin Place
North 39th Street
North 38th St
North 36th Street
North 35th Street
North 34th Street
North 34th
North Canal Street
Northlake Way
North Fremont Way
North Bridge Way
North Green
Aurora Avenue North
Fremont Avenue North
Phinney Avenue North
Greenwood Avenue North
Palatine Avenue North
Francis Avenue North
Dayton Avenue North
Evanston Avenue North
Linden Avenue North
Whitman Avenue North
Woodland Park Avenue North
Midvale Avenue North
Winslow Place North
Albion Place North
Allen
North West 50th St
North West 49th Street
North West 48th Street
North West 47th Street
North West 46th Street
North West 45th St
North West 44th Street
North West 43rd Street
North West 42nd Street
North West 40th Street
North West Bowdoin Place
North West 39th Street
N W 36th Street
North West Leary Way
North 51st Street
1st Avenue North West
2nd Avenue North West
3rd Avenue North West
4th Avenue North West
5th Avenue North West
Baker
Historic Ballard, Nordic Heritage Museum
BF Day Playground
Statue of Lenin
Fremont Sunday Market
Fremont Troll
History House
Waiting for the Interurban
Ballard Sunday Market, Fishermen's Memorial, Fishermen's Terminal, Discovery Park
Lake Washington Ship Canal
Fremont Bridge
George Washington Memorial Bridge (Aurora Bridge)
0
250 m
0
250 yds
2
3
4
5
6
A
B
C

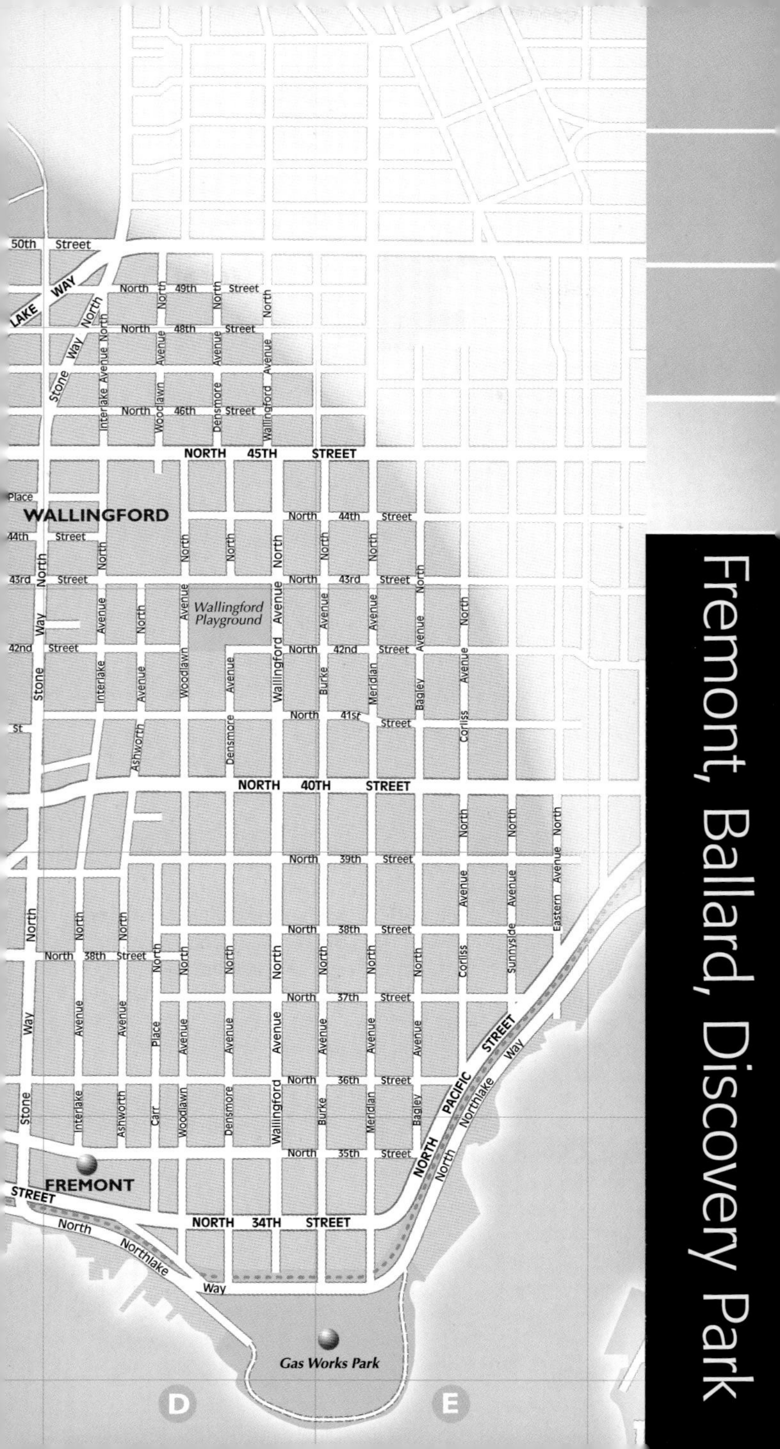
50th Street
LAKE WAY
North 49th Street
North 48th Street
North 46th Street
Stone Way
Interlake Avenue North
Woodlawn Avenue North
Densmore Avenue North
Wallingford Avenue North
NORTH 45TH STREET
Place
WALLINGFORD
44th Street
North 44th Street
43rd Street
North 43rd Street
Wallingford Playground
42nd Street
North 42nd Street
Burke Avenue North
Meridian Avenue North
Bagley Avenue North
Corliss Avenue North
North 41st Street
St
Ashworth
NORTH 40TH STREET
North 39th Street
North 38th Street
North 37th Street
North 36th Street
North 35th Street
Sunnyside Avenue North
Eastern Avenue North
Carr Place
NORTH PACIFIC STREET
North Northlake Way
FREMONT
STREET
NORTH 34TH STREET
Gas Works Park
D
E

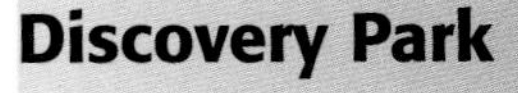

Discovery Park

TOP 25

DID YOU KNOW?

- Area: 534 acres (216ha).
- Bald eagles sometimes nest in the park.
- During World War II, the area was a major induction and training center for troops.

TIP

- If you're short on time but still want a good view of Puget Sound, park at the South Beach lot. From there, it's a short walk to the majestic West Point Light Station, a lighthouse built in 1881.

This park is the largest stand of wilderness in the city. Its meadows, forests, cliffs, marshes and shoreline provide habitat for many birds and animals.

Legacy of the military The 534 forested acres (216ha) on Magnolia Bluff that is today's Discovery Park was a military base from the 1890s, but in 1970 the government turned it over to the city for use as a park. During the transfer, an alliance of local tribes decided to take the opportunity to regain ancestral land they felt was theirs, and 20 acres (8ha) were set aside for a Native American cultural center.

Discover the trails The park's great size means that there are miles of nature and bike trails to be explored. Test your fitness along the

Where the waters of Puget Sound meet Discovery Park (left); children play in the water of the fountain (top right); Daybreak Star Arts Center, one of only four galleries dedicated to contemporary Native American art (bottom middle and right)

half-mile "parcours" (health path) through the woods. To the west, 2 miles (3km) of beach extend north and south from the West Point lighthouse (head south for sand, north for rocks). To get to the beach, pick up the loop trail at the north or south parking lot. The park's visitor center provides free 90-minute walks led by a naturalist, every Saturday at 2pm.

Daybreak Star Arts Center The structure uses enormous cedar timbers to reflect the points of a star. Native American art adorns the walls inside—the Arts Center is one of only four showcases dedicated to contemporary Native American work in the United States. Highlights of the collection include *The Earth is Our Mother* by Jimmie C. Fife and paintings by Robert Montoya.

THE BASICS

Discovery Park
www.seattle.gov/parks
Off map at A5
3801 W Government Way
206/386–4236
Park: daily dawn to dusk. Visitor center: daily 8.30–5 (except national holidays)
24, 33
Poor
Free

Daybreak Star Arts Center
206/285–4425
Mon–Fri 9–5
Very good
Salmon lunch/Artmart, Sat in Dec; Seafair Indian Pow-Wow Days, 3rd weekend in Jul

Hiram M. Chittenden Locks

TOP 25

DID YOU KNOW?

- Dedicated on July 4, 1917, the Locks were then the second-largest in the world.
- The locks enable vessels to be raised or lowered between 6 and 26ft (2 and 8m), as necessitated by the tides and lake level.
- The average passage through the large lock takes 25 minutes; 10 minutes through the small one.

TIPS

- It can be difficult to get in and out of the parking lot on weekends, but you might find street parking nearby.
- Usually, the peak time for boats to go through the locks is late morning.

Legions of boat owners pass through these locks when taking their boats from freshwater into Puget Sound. Alongside, salmon struggle to climb a fish ladder to return to their spawning grounds.

A dream comes true The 1917 opening of the Ballard Locks and Lake Washington Ship Canal was the fulfillment of a 60-year-old pioneer dream to build a channel that would link Lake Washington and Puget Sound. Primitive attempts were made in the 1880s, but it wasn't until Major Hiram M. Chittenden, regional director of the Army Corps of Engineers, won Congressional approval in 1909 that work began. Workers excavated and moved thousands of tons of earth with giant steam shovels. Displays in the visitor center explain the history of the locks and ship canal.

Part of the dramatic brushed stainless steel Salmon Waves *sculpture by Paul Storey, which adorns the lock side (right); the locks are operated from a control tower that regulates the spillway gates (below); the fish ladder (bottom right); leisure boats using the sea lock (bottom middle)*

Watch the fish A fish ladder, built into the locks, allows salmon and steelheads to move upstream from the sea to their spawning grounds. The fish find the narrow channel and begin the long journey to the freshwater spot where they began life. Here, they lay their eggs and die. There's a viewing window below the waterline, which is open year-round, but if you want to see the most activity visit in the spawning season. Sockeye head this way from about June through mid-August, while chinook and coho salmon follow in September, and you can observe steelheads right through the fall.

Botanical gardens Nearby, you can also explore the 7-acre (3ha) Carl S. English Jr. Botanical Gardens, which are planted with nearly 600 species from around the world.

THE BASICS

www.nws.usace.army.mil/Missions/CivilWorks/LocksandDams/ChittendenLocks.aspx

Off map at A2

3015 NW 54th Street

206/764–3464

Locks and gardens: daily 7am–9pm. Visitor center: May–Sep daily 10–6; Oct–Apr Thu–Mon 10–4. Fish Ladder Viewing Room daily 7am–8.45pm

17 from 4th Avenue

Very good Free

Public tours Mar–Nov (check online calendar for details)

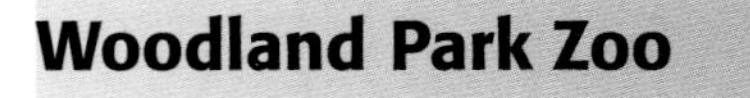

Woodland Park Zoo

TOP 25

DID YOU KNOW?

- Area: 92 acres (37ha).
- Woodland Park is the legacy of Guy Phinney, a savvy real estate developer who bought the land to build a country estate.
- In 1899, the city purchased Phinney's estate for $100,000.

TIP

- Bring binoculars—some of the exhibits are quite expansive. Don't miss the brown (grizzly) bear exhibit, which is among the world's best.

Woodland Park Zoo has won international recognition for its progressive design and is a highly respected leader in wildlife conservation. The animals move freely in settings that resemble their natural habitats.

Running free (almost) Most animals roam freely in their approximated "bioclimatic zones." Seven exhibits—African Savanna, Tropical Rain Forest, Northern Trail (Alaska), Humboldt Penguin, Jaguar Cove, Trail of Vines and Elephant Forest—have won prestigious awards and introduce visitors not only to the animals, but also to corresponding plant species and ecosystems. Other permanent exhibits include a southern African floodplain-riverbank habitat where rare African wildhogs live, the amazing replica of an African village, and

Take time out in the tranquil rose gardens at Woodland Park Zoo (top left); a jaguar cooling off in the water (bottom left); the giraffes (top right) and grizzly bears (bottom middle) are popular attractions; a plaque in the rose gardens dedicated to the efforts of the Lions Club and Seattle Rose Society (bottom right)

an exhibit of the rare Dragons of Komodo—the world's largest lizards. The Trail of Vines showcases macaques, tapirs, pythons and orangutans in a setting representing the forests of western India and northern Borneo.

Zoo newcomers The zoo has an active breeding program, so look out for new arrivals, which may include rare turtles, jaguar cubs, giraffes and komodo dragons.

Tours and treats The zoo offers myriad tours, programs and activities for visitors young and old. Some of the most popular include feeding times—especially the giraffes and elephants—and keeper talks at specific enclosures. The Real Close guided tours take you behind the scenes and get you closer to selected animals (book ahead).

THE BASICS

www.zoo.org
B2
5500 Phinney Avenue N
206/548–2500
May–Sep daily 9.30–6; Oct–Apr 9.30–4
Rain Forest Food Pavilion, Pacific Blue Chowder House
5, 44
Good
Expensive; half-price with purchase of CityPass
ZooTunes outdoor summer concerts on Wed nights, Jul–Aug

More to See

FISHERMEN'S MEMORIAL

Dominating the Fishermen's Terminal's central plaza, a 30ft (9m) high column commemorates those who lost their lives at sea.

Off map at A5 ✉ 3919 18th Avenue W at Salmon Bay 15 or 18 from 1st Avenue (exit south of Ballard Bridge)

FISHERMEN'S TERMINAL

Fishermen's Terminal is a great place to soak up the comings and goings of a large fleet. Fish have been an important local resource since Seattle's early days. In the early 1900s, a growing demand for salmon prompted the industry to lure new fishermen to the area—especially Scandinavian, Greek and Slavic immigrants—many of whose descendants still work in the fishing trade. Since 1913, this has been the home base for the North Pacific fishing fleet. Washington fishers harvest 40 percent of all fish and other seafood caught in the United States.

Off map at A5 ✉ 3919 18th Avenue W at Salmon Bay ☎ 206/728-3395 24 hours 15 or 18 from 1st Avenue (exit south of Ballard Bridge) Very good Free

FREMONT

www.fremont.com

This offbeat neighborhood, which proclaims itself a republic and "the Center of the Universe," is known for its tolerance and quirky humor. Check out the public art, from the monumental statue of Lenin to the Volkswagen-crushing *Fremont Troll* under Aurora Bridge.

D6 26, 28

FREMONT AND BALLARD SUNDAY MARKETS

Fresh produce, flowers, crafts, collectibles, antiques and plain old junk.

B5 ✉ Fremont neighborhood on N 34th between Stone Way and Fremont Avenue N May–end Oct Sun 10–4

GAS WORKS PARK

This park on north Lake Union is popular for picnics, kite-flying, skateboarding and wonderful views of

Fishing vessels gather in Fishermen's Terminal (left); the Fishermen's Memorial (right)

Shoppers hunting for a bargain at the Fremont Sunday market (below)

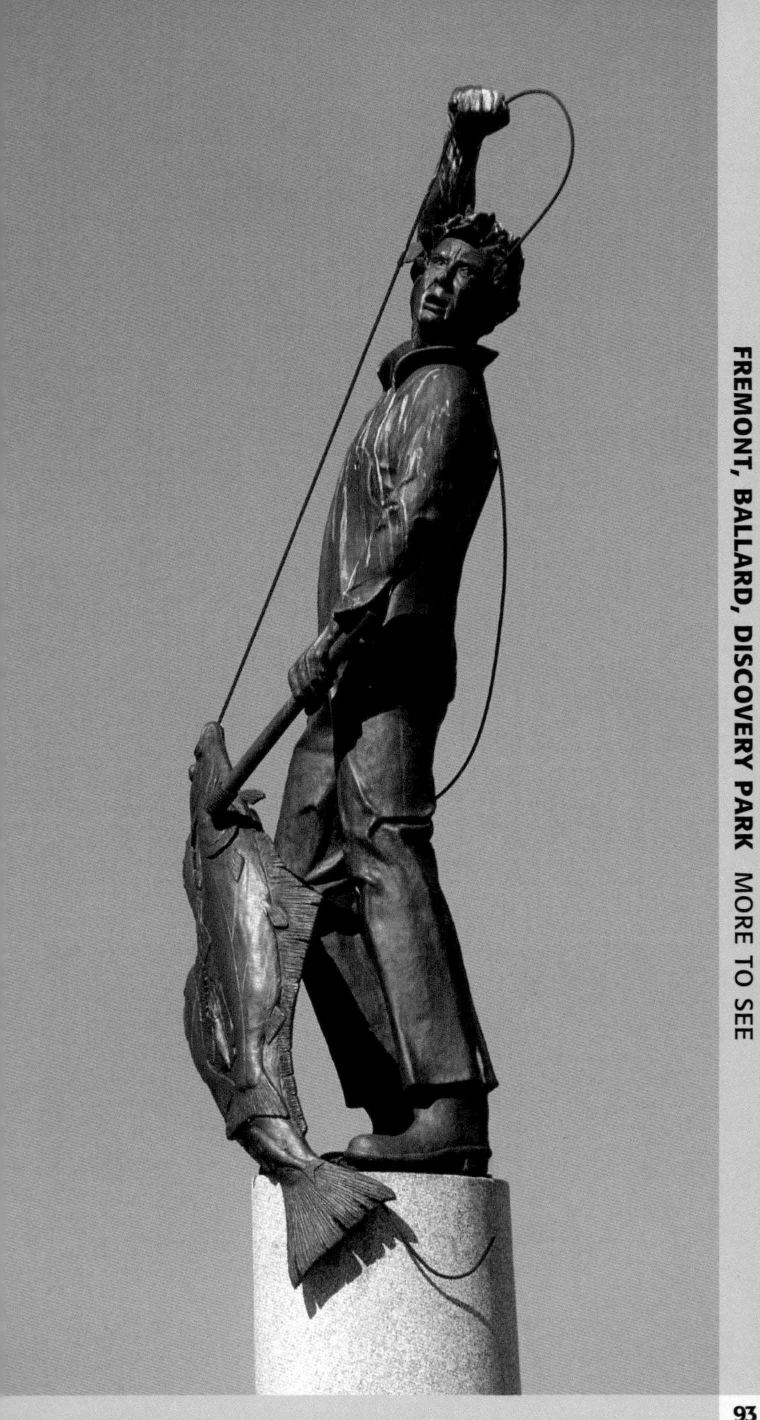

Downtown. Rusted, graffiti-marked towers and brightly painted machinery in the play area recall this site's origins as a gas plant. Climb the grassy mound to see the park's sundial or launch a kite.
E6 N Northlake Way and Meridian Avenue N 26

HISTORIC BALLARD

A former maritime center with a distinctive Scandinavian flavor, Ballard has evolved into a bustling urban village that still retains an atmosphere of home-grown hospitality. The landmark district is centered on Market Street and Ballard Avenue, with its beautifully restored 19th-century brick buildings. It's known for its burgeoning shopping, dining and entertainment scene.
Off map at A4 RapidRide D Line, 40, 61

HISTORY HOUSE

www.historyhouse.org
Depicts the history of the city's neighborhoods with photo displays, interactive kiosks and animated slide shows. Also a small sculpture garden.
C6 790 N 34th Street 206/675–8875 Wed–Sun 12–5

NORDIC HERITAGE MUSEUM

www.nordicmuseum.com
The only museum in the United States to showcase the heritage of all five Nordic nations: Denmark, Finland, Iceland, Norway and Sweden.
Off map at A4 3014 NW 67th Street 206/789–5707 Tue–Sat 10–4, Sun 12–4 17 (on 4th Avenue)
Inexpensive; free 1st Thu of month

WAITING FOR THE INTERURBAN

Richard Beyer's sculpture is a much-loved fixture of Fremont. Rarely are these gray aluminum trolley riders unadorned, either with scarves and hats in winter, or at other times through the year with balloons and banners to acknowledge someone's birthday.
B6 Fremont Avenue N and N 34th Street 26, 28

Myths and legends are realized in stone: the Fremont Troll

Shopping

LES AMIS

www.lesamis-inc.com

This rustic boutique is home to some fantastic frocks designed by the likes of Rozae Nichols, Diane Von Furstenburg and Trina Turk.

Off map 3420 Evanston Avenue N 206/632-2877 Mon–Sat 11–6, Sun 11–5

ARTFX

www.artfx.net

More than 100 local artists and craftspeople are represented by this gallery, which includes paintings, prints, sculpture, jewelry and more.

B5 402 N 35th Street 206/545-7459 Thu–Sun 12–5

FREMONT VINTAGE MALL

www.fremontvintagemall.com

Fifty different dealers share this rambling space in Fremont and sell everything from clothes, antiques and collectibles to records and toys. Visit the Macabre Corner for strange items like a William Burroughs finger painting.

B5 3419 Fremont Place N 206/548-9140 Mon–Sat 11–7, Sun 11–6

GOLD DOGS VINTAGE

There's a huge variety of clothing for men and women, footwear, bags jewelry and accessories, and the staff is super-helpful.

B5 3519 Fremont Place N 206/499-1811 Daily 12–6

HUB AND BESPOKE

www.hubandbespoke.com

If you ride a bike, you'll love this shop, with a range of bike-friendly clothing plus accessories.

B5 513 N 36th Street 206/547-5730 Mon, Wed, Thu 12–7, Fri–Sat 12–6

PORTAGE BAY GOODS

www.portagebaygoods.com

Environmentally friendly gifts by local and world-wide artisans.

B6 621 N 35th Street 206/547-5221 Daily 10–7

FREMONT FUNK

With *De Libertas Quirkas* (the right to be quirky) as its motto, it's no wonder that Seattle's Fremont neighborhood is both the birthplace and breeding ground of local funk. In the 1960s and 1970s artists, bohemians and students began moving into old brick buildings that had fallen into disrepair. Attracted by low rents, these new residents set up studios, shops and cafés that established a playful, down-home aesthetic. Before long, they'd formed the Fremont Arts Council, charged with helping create a sense of community through art—and not the highbrow art of cultural institutions but accessible art with a sense of humor. Their concept of art embraced whimsical public sculptures like *Waiting for the Interurban*, and the *Fremont Troll*.

RE-SOUL

www.resoul.com

An eclectic blend of shoes, artwork, jewelry and home furnishings.

Off map 5319 Ballard Avenue NW 206/789-7312 Mon–Sat 11–8, Sun 11–5

SHOW PONY BOUTIQUE

www.showponyboutique.com

This sister to the Los Angeles store sells new and consignment clothing, shoes, jewelry, accessories and perfume for women.

B5 702 N 35th Street 206/706-4188 Mon–Sat 11–7, Sun 11–5

THEO CHOCOLATE

www.theochocolate.com

You can take a factory tour here, or just visit the shop for some of their delectable hand-crafted, organic, Fair Trade confections.

B5 3400 Phinney Avenue N 206/632-5100 Daily 10–6

THISTLE ACCESSOIRE

www.thistleaccessoire.com

Pretty up your outfit here with a selection of scarves, bags and jewelry.

B5 617 N 35th Street 206/632-2626 Mon–Wed 11–6, Thu–Sat 11–7, Sun 11–5

Restaurants

PRICES

Prices are approximate, based on a 3-course meal for one person.
$$$ over $50
$$ $30–$50
$ under $30

ANTHONY'S HOMEPORT ($$)
www.anthonys.com
Airy and attractive restaurant with waterfront views and fresh seafood.
Off map 6135 Seaview NW, Shilshole
206/783–0780

BALLARD ANNEX OYSTER HOUSE ($$)
www.ballardannex.com
House-made chowder is a good prelude to the fresh seafood—oysters, Dungeness crab, Maine lobster, beer-battered fish and chips, salmon and more.
Off map 5410 Ballard Avenue NW 206/783–5410 Mon–Thu 3.30–11, Fri–Sat 11–midnight, Sun 11–11

CAFÉ BESALU ($)
The pastries here are absolutely to die for. Don't miss the ginger biscuits.
Off map 5909 24th Avenue NW 206/789–1463 Wed–Sun 7–3

EL CAMINO ($$)
www.elcaminorestaurant.com
Lively crowds pack this Fremont neighborhood spot for Mexican fare and tasty margaritas.
B5 607 N 35th Street 206/632–7303 Dinner nightly; closed Labor Day

CANLIS ($$$)
www.canlis.com
Excellent Northwest fare with Asian accents. A special-occasion eatery.
C7 2576 Aurora Avenue N 206/283–3313 Dinner Mon–Sat

HATTIE'S HAT ($)
www.hatties-hat.com
A Seattle institution since who-knows-when, this joint is known for its classic American menu and its hand-carved bar.
Off map 5231 Ballard Avenue NW 206/784–0175 Lunch and dinner daily, breakfast Sat, Sun

HERKIMER COFFEE ($)
An excellent place for a morning coffee and a newspaper. Smart, clean interior and a friendly staff make this spot a neighborhood treasure.
Off map 7320 Greenwood Avenue N
206/784–0202
Mon–Fri 6–6, Sat, Sun 7–6

FARMERS' MARKET

During the summertime, Ballard's Sunday farmers' market is a draw for foodies from all over the city—fresh produce, cheeses, meats, flowers and much more.
Off map 5330 Ballard Avenue NW 206/781–6776 Apr–Nov Sun 10–3

MAD PIZZA ($)
www.madpizza.com
Come here for some of the city's best pizza.
B5 N 36th Avenue (west of Fremont Avenue N)
206/632–5453

RAY'S BOATHOUSE ($$$)
www.rays.com
A to-die-for view and dependably good seafood at this lively fish house. The upstairs café offers a waterside outdoor deck—and people-watching.
Off map 6049 Seaview Avenue NW 206/789–3770 Lunch and dinner daily

STAPLE & FANCY ($$$)
www.ethanstowellrestaurants.com
As the name implies, you can choose Italian staples or a fancy multi-course feast from the kitchen of James Beard-Award-winning chef Ethan Stowell.
Off map 4739 Ballard Avenue NW 206/789–1200 Dinner daily

STUMBLING GOAT BISTRO ($$)
www.stumblinggoatbistro.com
With a menu heavy on local produce and meats and a chef with an all-star culinary pedigree, this candle-lit bistro is a delight.
Off map 6722 Greenwood Avenue N
206/784–3535
Dinner Tue–Sun

Farther Afield

One of Seattle's greatest attributes is its proximity to towering mountains, sparkling waterways and old-growth forests. The region is also blessed with picturesque rural towns and ideal day-trip destinations.

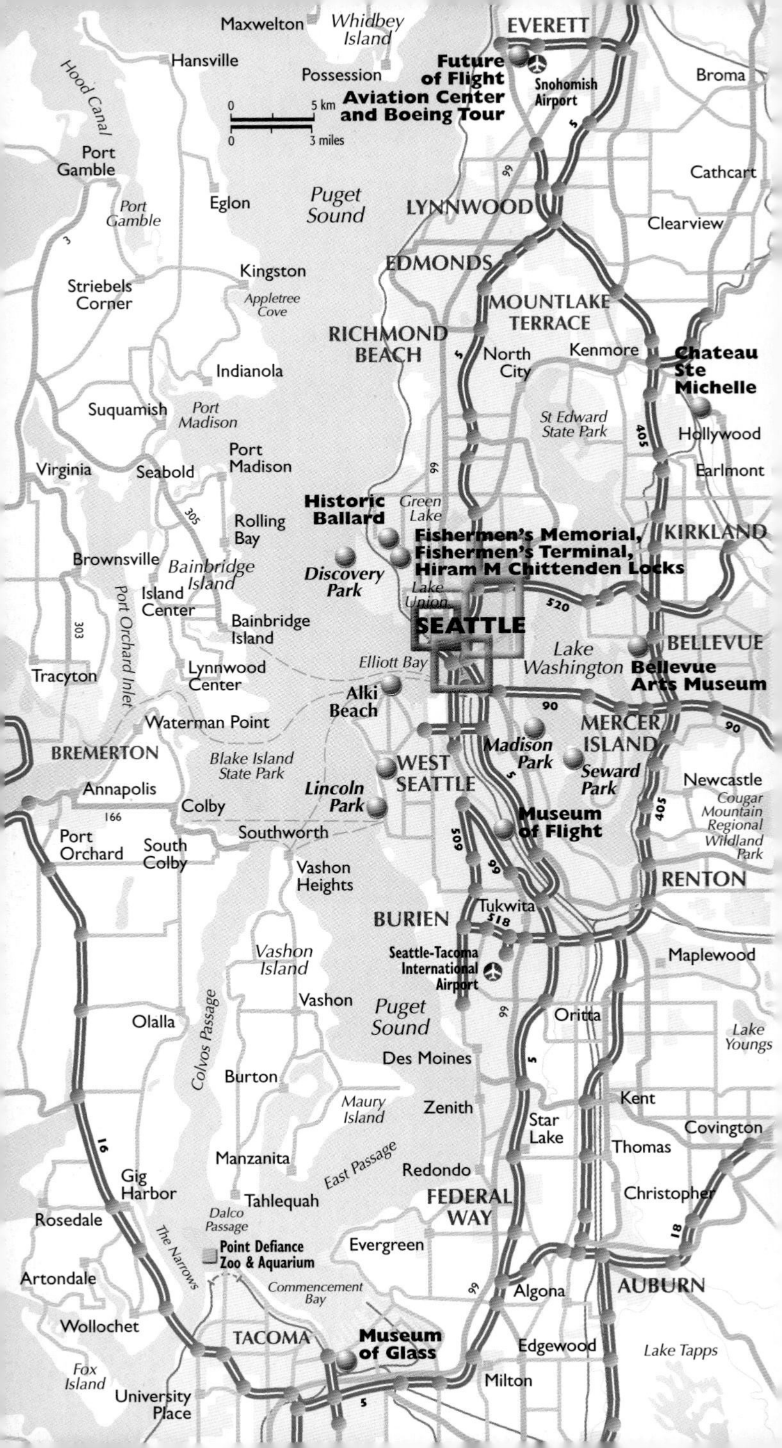

Maxwelton
Whidbey Island
EVERETT
Hansville
Hood Canal
Possession
Future of Flight Aviation Center and Boeing Tour
Snohomish Airport
Broma
0 5 km
0 3 miles
Port Gamble
Eglon
Port Gamble
Puget Sound
LYNNWOOD
Cathcart
Clearview
EDMONDS
Kingston
Appletree Cove
Striebels Corner
MOUNTLAKE TERRACE
RICHMOND BEACH
North City
Kenmore
Chateau Ste Michelle
Indianola
Suquamish
Port Madison
St Edward State Park
Hollywood
Port Madison
Virginia
Seabold
Earlmont
Historic Ballard
Green Lake
Rolling Bay
Fishermen's Memorial, Fishermen's Terminal, Hiram M Chittenden Locks
KIRKLAND
Brownsville
Bainbridge Island
Discovery Park
Island Center
Port Orchard Inlet
Lake Union
Bainbridge Island
SEATTLE
BELLEVUE
Lake Washington
Bellevue Arts Museum
Elliott Bay
Tracyton
Lynnwood Center
Alki Beach
Waterman Point
MERCER ISLAND
BREMERTON
Madison Park
Seward Park
Blake Island State Park
WEST SEATTLE
Newcastle
Annapolis
Lincoln Park
Cougar Mountain Regional Wildland Park
Colby
Museum of Flight
Port Orchard
South Colby
Southworth
Vashon Heights
RENTON
BURIEN
Tukwila
Seattle-Tacoma International Airport
Maplewood
Vashon Island
Vashon
Puget Sound
Olalla
Oritta
Lake Youngs
Colvos Passage
Des Moines
Burton
Kent
Maury Island
Zenith
Star Lake
Covington
Thomas
Manzanita
East Passage
Redondo
Gig Harbor
FEDERAL WAY
Christopher
Tahlequah
Rosedale
Dalco Passage
Point Defiance Zoo & Aquarium
Evergreen
The Narrows
Artondale
Commencement Bay
Algona
AUBURN
Wollochet
TACOMA
Museum of Glass
Edgewood
Lake Tapps
Fox Island
Milton
University Place
5
99
405
520
90
305
303
3
166
16
509
518
18

Farther Afield

Alki Beach and West Seattle

TOP 25

HIGHLIGHTS

- Pickup games of beach volleyball
- Driftwood beach fires at sunset
- People-watching on the crowded promenade
- Amazing views of Downtown

TIP

- There's only limited street parking at the beach. The water taxi from Downtown to West Seattle is a good (and scenic) alternative.

Alki Beach is Seattle's birthplace. Today, its sandy shore and waterfront trail are as close as Seattle gets to resembling Southern California.

Beginnings The Duwamish and Suquamish peoples were on hand to meet the schooner *Exact* when it sailed into Elliott Bay on November 13, 1851. The ship anchored off Alki Point and Arthur Denny and his party of 23 paddled their skiff ashore. The locals proved friendly and the Denny party decided to stay. They set about building four log cabins, wistfully naming their new home New York–Alki, "Alki" being a word in the Chinook language for "someday," an indication of Denny's ambitions. The following year, after surviving fierce winter storms, the settlers decided to move across

The whitewashed Alki Point Light Station safeguards against any dangers on Puget Sound (left, bottom right); children paddling in the waters of Puget Sound off Alki Beach (top middle); the beautiful sandy shoreline (bottom middle); the grassy areas stretching alongside Alki Beach are popular with picnickers (top right)

Elliott Bay to the more sheltered, deepwater harbor that is today's Pioneer Square.

Beach life The beach itself is the main attraction today. There are great views, fine sand, a paved trail and boat and bike rentals. There's food and drink, too—try Pegasus (for pizza) or the Alki Café Beach Bistro. You can walk, bike or skate the 2.5 miles (4km) from Alki Beach to Duwamish Head. Continue south along the water to lovely Lincoln Park, where there is an outdoor saltwater pool and waterslide.

Scuba in Seattle Alki Beach is a popular destination for Seattle's diehard divers. Most dive at the eastern end of the beach, not far from Salty's restaurant. The water temperature ranges from 46 to 56°F (8 to 14°C).

THE BASICS

See map ▷ 98
3201 Alki Avenue SW (Alki Point Light Station)
206/684–4075
Lighthouse Sat–Sun 1–4. Coast Guard officer on duty Jun–Aug
37, 56, 57
Kings County Water Taxi from Seacrest Park downtown (Mon–Sat)
Wheelchair access
Bike, inline skate and boat rentals; driftwood fires permitted on beach

Future of Flight Aviation Center and Boeing Tour

TOP 25

A Boeing 787 in production (right); the finished article rolls out of the Boeing factory (left)

THE BASICS

www.futureofflight.org
See map ▷ 98
8415 Paine Field Boulevard, Mukilteo
206/544–1264 (recorded information); 800/464–1476
Future of Flight: daily 8.30–5.30; tours 9–3 on the hour
Very good
Expensive
Height restriction on tour for children 4ft (122cm). Same-day tickets sold on-site on first-come first-served basis

DID YOU KNOW?

- The aircraft assembly building is so huge that it developed an interior weather system in which rain clouds would form. A special air circulation system now controls the climate.
- Workers use bicycles to get around the factory floor.
- The Boeing plant covers 98.3 acres (40ha) under one roof.

Over the years, Seattle's fortunes have soared and dipped on the wings of Boeing. Take a tour of this magnificent factory and discover what lies ahead.

A century of growth 2016 marks the 100th anniversary of the first airplane manufactured by William Boeing and his partner, Conrad Westerveld—the B&W. Out of that venture grew the multinational Boeing corporation and this vast production facility 30 minutes north of Seattle. The world's largest building measured by volume (more than 3 cubic miles/13 cubic km), it's on the go 24 hours a day, with thousands of workers assembling 747s, 777s and 787 Dreamliners.

Future of flight A truly interactive experience is offered at this forward-looking center, including the chance to try out a Dreamliner interior and offer your opinions to the research team. After exploring all aspects of airplane design, you can digitally design your own—at last, more legroom—then operate a virtual test flight on a touch-screen computer. Sit in a flight deck, peer into jet engines, learn about advances in sustainable fuels and look into the airborne future.

The tour The 90-minute Boeing tour begins with a short film. Afterward, a guide takes you to the plant's third floor, where an observation deck provides a view of the final assembly operation. Outside, you are shown where the painting, fueling and ground testing of the aircraft occurs.

Two of the many exhibits proudly presented at the Museum of Flight

TOP 25 Museum of Flight

This stunning building is one of the largest and finest air and space museums in the world. Even technophobes will be engaged and delighted.

Red Barn and Air Park This is where Boeing's first planes were built, and displays cover the company's history and early days of flight. You'll get to know the Wright brothers and see a model of their 1903 Flyer. Outside, in the Airpark, you can visit six of the largest aircraft, including the first jet Air Force One and a Concorde.

Great Gallery and Space Gallery The airy and breathtaking Great Gallery traces the story of flight from early mythology to the latest accomplishments in space. Overhead, more than 20 full-size airplanes hang at varying levels from a ceiling grid. All face the same direction, like a squadron frozen in flight. Altogether there are more than 150 iconic air and space craft on display. Another exhibit contains objects from the Apollo space program, including an Apollo command module, lunar rocks and the Lunar Roving Vehicle. You can also see the NASA Space Shuttle Trainer in which every Shuttle astronaut honed their skills.

Control the traffic Using the latest technology, the Flight Tower simulates the work of air traffic controllers and their communications with pilots, but it gets real too. You can view the King County International Airport and hear live communications with incoming flights.

THE BASICS

www.museumofflight.org

See map ▷ 98

9404 E Marginal Way S by Boeing Field

206/764-5720

Daily 10–5 (1st Thu of month until 9)

Wings Café

124

Excellent

Expensive. Free 1st Thu of month, 5–9pm

Family workshops; special events

HIGHLIGHTS

- A restored 1917 Curtiss "Jenny" biplane
- A flying replica of the B&W, Boeing's first plane
- The only MD-21 Blackbird spy plane in existence
- Apollo space program objects
- A full-size air traffic control tower
- Piloting an imaginary flight
- NASA Space Shuttle Trainer

More to See

BELLEVUE ARTS MUSEUM (BAM)
www.bellevuearts.org
Across Lake Washington on Seattle's Eastside, BAM shows contemporary visual art, craft and design of the Northwest. The building's sculptural qualities and architect Stephen Holl's use of natural light have created a luminous space that both explores and generates art.
See map ▷ 98 ✉ 510 Bellevue Way NE ☎ 425/519–0770 Tue–Sun 10–6 (1st Fri until 8) 550 from bus tunnel Moderate

CHATEAU STE. MICHELLE
www.ste-michelle.com
Daily tours and wine tastings are held from10 to 5. Reservations and a small fee are required for special vintage-reserve tastings.
See map ▷ 98 ✉ 14111 NE 145th Street in Woodinville, NE of Seattle ☎ 425/488–1133 255 to Kirkland, then 236 to Woodville Free

LINCOLN PARK
A lovely West Seattle park south of Alki with something for everyone: great views, rocky beaches with tide-pools, walking and biking trails, picnic shelters, tennis courts, a horseshoe pit, a saltwater pool and waterslide.
See map ▷ 98 ✉ Fauntleroy Avenue SW and SW Webster 54

MUSEUM OF GLASS
www.museumofglass.org
South of Seattle lies Tacoma, home of glass artist Dale Chihuly (▷ 48), where this dazzling Museum of Glass occupies 13,000sq ft (3,963sq m) of exhibition space. The glass-walled concrete structure incorporates in its design a 90ft (27m) steel cone housing the Hot Shop, where you can watch glassworkers shape enormous molten globs into art. A dramatic glass bridge connects the museum to the Washington State History Museum.
See map ▷ 98 ✉ 1801 Dock Street, Tacoma ☎ 253/284–4750 or 866/468–7386 Late May–early Sep Mon–Sat 10–5, Sun 12–5; early Sep–late May Wed–Sat 10–5, Sun 12–5 (3rd Thu 10–8) Prizm Café Sounder train Sound Transit #594 Moderate

Bellevue Arts Museum

HURRICANE RIDGE/ OLYMPIC NATIONAL PARK

Olympic National Park is one of the nation's most diverse parks; its boundaries encompass remote ocean beaches, primeval temperate rain forests and high alpine glaciers and ridgelines.

Hurricane Ridge rises nearly a vertical mile above Port Angeles and the northern end of the Olympic Peninsula. When the sun graces its slopes, the Ridge's visitors enjoy endless views of the Strait of Juan de Fuca, Vancouver Island and beyond. A visitor center greets you at the summit and a series of nature trails provide ample opportunities for hiking. Sure, the drive from Seattle is significant, but the variety of wild spaces you'll encounter make the trip well worth it. Don't forget your raincoat, though.

THE BASICS

Distance: 100 miles (160km) northwest of Seattle
Journey Time: 3 hours by road and Washington State Ferry
Route: I–5 north to Edmonds; take the ferry to Kingston; west on 104 to 101; north on 101 to Port Angeles; south on Hurricane Ridge Road to visitor center
Bus Tours: Viator ☎ 360/417–8006
Olympic National Park: ☎ 702/648–5873 or 888/651–9785
Hurricane Ridge Visitor Center: ☎ 360/565–3131

MOUNT RAINIER

Mt. Rainier, one of a string of active volcanoes running south from the Canadian border to California, rises 14,410ft (4,392m) above sea level, and the upper 6,000ft (1,800m) are covered in snow year-round.

On clear days, the mountain's white dome, apparently hovering over Seattle, has an appearance so awesome and so immediate that it's hard to believe it's actually 90 miles (145km) away. Small wonder that native peoples ascribed supernatural power to the mountain. For a closer view of Mount Rainier's peak, drive to Crystal Mountain and take the chairlift to its summit. For information on hiking, stop at Longmire, then drive on for 11 miles (18km) to the Henry M. Jackson Memorial Visitor Center at Paradise, where many of the trails begin.

THE BASICS

Distance: 90 miles (145km) southeast of Seattle
Journey Time: 3 hours by road
Route: I–5 south to Tacoma; east on route 512; south on route 7 and east on route 706 to the park entrance
Bus Tours: Gray Line (▷ 119); Tours Northwest ☎ 888/293-1404; Mt. Rainier Tours ☎ 253/777-8226
Mt. Rainier National Park: ☎ 360/569–2211; www.nps.org/mora
Paradise Visitor Center: ☎ 360/569–6571

THE BASICS

Journey Time: 2.5–3 hours by boat
Victoria Clipper, Pier 69 ☎ 206/448–500 or 800/888–2535; **www.**clippervacations.com/seattle-victoria-ferry/
Enquire for schedule
A visit to Victoria means crossing the border into Canada, so you'll need to take your passport and other necessary travel documents

VICTORIA, BRITISH COLUMBIA

British Columbia's capital city is a verdant paradise complete with year-round flowers, gorgeous architecture and a historical downtown seaport.

With its many festivals and holiday celebrations, the city honors its cultural influences, both British and Native. High-speed catamarans cruise Puget Sound and the Strait of Juan de Fuca, and sail into Victoria, Canada, for a taste of merry England (with formal gardens, double-decker buses and shops selling tweeds and Irish linen). At the Royal British Columbia Museum you can view items made by Native Americans living on the Northwest Coast. Take a bus to the beautiful Butchart Gardens or indulge yourself with tea in the imperial splendor of the Empress Hotel.

THE BASICS

Distance: 30 miles (50km) northwest of Seattle
Journey Time: 1.5 hours by road and Washington State Ferry
Route: I–5 north to Mukilteo; take ferry to Clinton; west on 525 to Langley, Freeland and Coupeville
Langley: ☎ 360/221–6765; www.visitlangley.com
Coupeville: ☎ 360/678–5434; **www.**cometocoupeville.com
Ebey's Landing: ☎ 360/678–6084; **www.**nps.gov/ebla

WHIDBEY ISLAND

Lying 30 miles (50km) northwest of Seattle, Whidbey Island is a bucolic counterpoint to the city's hustle and bustle and is a popular retreat for city dwellers.

Dotted with farms, lush forests, small towns, country roads and sandy beaches, the island has an active, vibrant community of its own. Whidbey is approximately 60 miles (100km) long, and in many places it's less than 2 miles (3km) in width. The north end of the island is dominated by a naval base and the associated city of Oak Harbor, but the south end is far more scenic. Of particular note are the communities of Langley and Coupeville, both of which have historic downtowns, excellent restaurants and shopping, and top-flight bed and breakfast inns. Ebey's Landing National Historical Reserve is one of the Puget Sound's most beautiful waterfront parks, and it shouldn't be passed over.

Where to Stay

You're bound to find the perfect place to rest your head in this city, where lodgings run the gamut from berths on a boat to hip hotels and the very best in luxury. Many hotels Downtown even throw in a great view of Puget Sound, as well.

Introduction

Seattle is home to a wide range of lodging choices, including luxury boutique hotels, major chains, bed and breakfasts and everything in between.

Budget or Luxury?

There are a number of inexpensive chain hotels in the city, as well as more than a few independent budget properties. Seattle also has a smattering of B&Bs and just a few hostels—unusual for a city of this size. There are several hotels competing for high-end visitors and most pull out all the stops to impress their guests. These hotels are centered around the Downtown area and rarely disappoint.

Where to Stay

The majority of the city's hotels are in and around Downtown, but accommodations can be found in all outlying neighborhoods. The bustling University District is not a bad place to stay, considering the proximity to the city, and the hotels here are less expensive than those Downtown. Although the waterfront is a tourist hot spot, it is not the easiest place to find a hotel. Bordering the eastern edge of Lake Union, Eastlake offers moderately priced, large residence-style hotels, and is still convenient for the city. Bellevue and the Eastside, across Lake Washington, are ideal spots for visitors who don't mind a short commute; the lodgings here range in quality and price and are convenient to business and shopping. If you prefer not to stray far from Sea-Tac Airport (about half an hour from Downtown), there are plenty of options—if you don't mind the plane noise.

DISCOUNTS

Many of the larger hotels and some smaller ones offer special corporate rates or discounts. Some hotels catering to business travelers may have reduced rates on weekends; in addition, most establishments lower their rates in the off-season. Discount web services such as www.hotels.com, www.priceline.com and www.hotwire.com can also present excellent deals.

Budget Hotels

PRICES

Expect to pay under $130 for a double room per night in a budget hotel.

BED & BREAKFAST INN

www.seattlebednbreakfast.com

Perks at this Capitol Hill B&B include off-street parking, free WiFi and a generous breakfast buffet with organic local ingredients. Rooms vary in size, but all are cozy with a dock for your iPod.

H12 1808 E Denny Way 206/412-7378 (10-6 only) or 206/323-1955 8, 12

CITY HOSTEL

www.hostelseattle.com

Local artists decorated the rooms in this Belltown hostel—it's fun, but don't expect a serene color scheme. Small dorms sleep four or six. Private rooms have shared or private bathrooms.

C3 2327 2nd Avenue 206/706-3255 or 1-877/HOSTEL 5 Central Link to Westlake

COLLEGE INN GUEST HOUSE

www.collegeinnseattle.com

The upper floors of this 1904 Tudor-style building house a pension with 25 rooms, each with a bed, wash basin, writing desk and shared bathroom. A continental breakfast is served and there is a café and pub downstairs.

H14 4000 University Way NE 206/633-4441

GEORGETOWN INN

www.georgetowninnseattle.com

Between Downtown and the airport in historic Georgetown, this hotel has simple but good-size rooms, with TV, air-conditioning, high-speed Internet and a mini-fridge. A continental breakfast is served. Free parking.

Off map 6100 Corson Avenue S 206/762-2233 106, 124

GREEN TORTOISE HOSTEL

www.greentortoise.net

Centrally located at the Pike Place Market. Thirty-seven rooms, shared and private: linen provided. Shared kitchen, and common room with stereo and TV; lockers and laundry facilities. Free Internet service, free breakfast, area discount card, 24-hour check-in.

D14 105 Pike Street 206/340-1222 or 888/424-6783 Free bus zone

B&B ASSOCIATION

The Seattle Bed & Breakfast Association represents independently owned, inspected B&Bs and inns, with members in and around Seattle, but all within 30 minutes of the airport. Their website has information and links to member websites.

206/547-1020; www.lodgingsinseattle.com

HOTEL HOTEL

www.hotelhotel.co

Part hotel, part hostel, in the heart of Fremont, this stylish place has dorms accommodating eight, double rooms (with or without private bathroom) and family rooms.

C3 3515 Fremont Avenue N 206/257-4543 26, 28, 40

KINGS INN

www.kingsinnseattle.com

Friendly staff, 68 rooms and a great Downtown location across from the monorail. Cable TV, laundry. Free parking.

D13 2106 5th Avenue 800/546-4760

MOORE HOTEL

www.moorehotel.com

This budget hotel is in the same building as the legendary Moore Theater. All rooms have private bathrooms, and the Downtown location is tough to beat.

D14 1926 2nd Avenue 206/448-4851 10, 12, 15, 18

UNIVERSITY HOTEL

www.university-hotel.com

Large suites on a quiet street in the University district. Each unit has separate bedrooms with kitchen. Plain furnishings, but good space and free parking.

G4 4731 12th Avenue 206/522-4724

Mid-Range Hotels

PRICES

Expect to pay between $130 and $250 per night for a double room in a mid-range hotel.

11TH AVENUE INN

www.11thavenueinn.com

An attractive B&B on the west slope of Capitol Hill, close to Downtown. Rooms include queen beds, down comforters, cable TV, wireless Internet, two guest computers and free local calls—including free long-distance (within US/Canada) telephone service in the den.

G16 121 11th Avenue E 206/720-7161 8, 9, 60

ACE HOTEL

www.theacehotel.com

This affordable and stylish Belltown hotel features futuristic lines in its 28 whitewashed rooms, each with high ceilings, hardwood floors and a sink and vanity; some with private bathrooms. It attracts those looking for good value.

C13 2423 1st Avenue 206/448-4721

BACON MANSION

www.baconmansion.com

This 11-room B&B is in a beautiful Capitol Hill Tudor-style home that was built in 1909. Many rooms feature private baths. Complimentary WiFi access throughout.

G14 959 Broadway E 206/329-1864 25, 49

BEST WESTERN EXECUTIVE INN

Close to Seattle Center, north of Downtown. Guest rooms at this major chain hotel feature Hypnos pillowtop beds and cable or satellite TV. An on-site restaurant and lounge serves breakfast, lunch and dinner.

C12 200 Taylor Avenue N 206/448-9444 3, 4, 16 Monorail to Downtown

GASLIGHT INN

www.gaslight-inn.com

Lovingly restored turn-of-the-20th-century mansion and annex. Fifteen well-appointed rooms, charming courtyard with plants and a small swimming pool.

H13 1727 15th Avenue 206/325-3654 10, 43

LODGING GUIDES

- The Seattle tourist organization's website, www.visitseattle.org, includes a hotel guide and the Hotel Concierge booking service, offering deals and discounts.
- The Pacific Reservation Service has a website at www.seattlebedandbreakfast.com. Click on "Find the Perfect Place" and then select from a list of options to find appealing lodgings in residential areas.
- Try calling the Seattle Hotel Hotline (800/535-7071 or 866/732-2695) for help with last-minute hotel reservations.

HAMPTON INN DOWNTOWN

www.hamptoninn.com

This motor inn at Seattle Center has an attractive lobby and 124 comfortable rooms. Continental breakfast, 24-hour fitness room. Free parking.

C11 700 5th Avenue N 206/282-7700 or 800/HAMPTON 3, 4, 16 Monorail to Downtown

HAWTHORN INN AND SUITES

www.hawthorn.com

Between Downtown and Seattle Center, this hotel has 72 rooms. Free local calls and free parking. Complimentary breakfast, sauna and spa, fitness room and free bike rental.

D12 2224 8th Avenue 206/624-6820 or 800/437-4867

HOTEL ANDRA

www.hotelandra.com

Andra pushes the boundary of a mid-range—many would call it luxury. This Scandinavian-influenced hotel has 119 rooms and suites, all of which are decorated with a minimalist modern aesthetic. The result: a visually stunning, comfortable retreat in the heart of Downtown.

D14 2000 4th Avenue

206/448-8600
1, 2, 4, 5 and many others

HOTEL MAX

www.hotelmaxseattle.com
Swanky, ultramodern hotel featuring more than 350 pieces of original art by local artists. Rooms have thick pillowtop mattresses, plush robes, gourmet coffees and teas, private bars and even a menu from which to select your favorite pillows.
D13 620 Stewart Street 206/728-6299 or 866/833-6299 1, 2, 4, 5 and many others

HOTEL SEATTLE

www.thehotelseattle.com
Downtown hotel with 81 rooms. The restaurant/lounge serves breakfast and lunch.
E15 315 Seneca
206/623-5110 or 800/426-2439

HOTEL VINTAGE

www.hotelvintageseattle.com
A lovely Downtown boutique hotel with a wine-theme decor. Each room is dedicated to a local winery or vineyard. Amenities galore, including 24-hour room service, a nightly wine reception in the lobby and soundproof windows.
E15 1100 5th Avenue
206/624-8000
1, 2, 4, 5 and many others

INN AT QUEEN ANNE

www.innatqueenanne.com
Comfortable 68-room inn in an older brick building next to Seattle Center. Complimentary breakfast, kitchenettes, cable TV, voicemail and air-conditioning.
B12 1st Avenue N 206/282-7357 or 800/952-5043
1, 2, 13, 15, 18

INN OF TWIN GABLES

www.innoftwingables.com
Yet another impressive urban B&B. On the west slope of Queen Anne Hill, this inn offers good access to Ballard, Fremont, Queen Anne and Downtown. Personal service, luxurious rooms and fresh flowers.
Off map 3528 14th Avenue W 206/284-3258
1, 2, 3, 15, 18

MAYFLOWER PARK

www.mayflowerpark.com
An elegant hotel with 172 rooms in a renovated 1920s building near Westlake Center. Home of the Andaluca Restaurant.
D14 405 Olive Way
206/623-8700 or 800/426-5100

RATES

Like their counterparts in most American cities, Seattle's hotels continually adjust their rates to accommodate customer demand. To get the best rate, don't be afraid to call the hotel itself; ask about special rates or discounts (▷ 108). Remember that local taxes will be added to your bill. The city has lots of rooms across all price points, but comfortable rooms are rarely less than $160.

SILVER CLOUD INN–LAKE UNION

www.silvercloud.com
Opened 2003, this inn has 184 well-appointed guest rooms featuring high-speed Internet connection. Other facilities include complimentary breakfast and airport shuttle, a concierge service, outdoor pool, fitness room and sauna.
E10 1150 Fairview Avenue N 206/447-9500 or 800/330-5812

SILVER CLOUD INN–UNIVERSITY

www.silvercloud.com
This inn has 180 units with mini-kitchens. Swimming pool, fitness center, complimentary continental breakfast.
J2 5036 25th Avenue NE 206/526-5200 or 800/205-6940

WATERTOWN HOTEL

www.watertownseattle.com
This inviting small hotel, within walking distance of the university, offers attractive studios or suites with large bathrooms and Internet access.
G3 4242 Roosevelt Way NE 206/826-4242 or 866/944-4242

Luxury Hotels

PRICES

Expect to pay over $250 per night for a double room at a luxury hotel.

ALEXIS HOTEL

www.alexishotel.com
Small Downtown hotel with tasteful postmodern styling and impeccable service; 109 guest rooms.
D15 1007 1st Avenue 206/624-4844 or 800/426-7033

FAIRMONT OLYMPIC HOTEL

www.fairmont.com
Many consider this elegant 450-room hotel Seattle's finest. Built in 1924, it offers a fitness center, pool, shops and restaurants, including the lavish Georgian Room.
E15 411 University Street 206/621-1700

FOUR SEASONS

www.fourseasons.com/seattle
With wonderful views and a central Downtown location, this is a contemporary high-rise hotel, enhanced by displays of local art. Rooms are spacious, with light flooding in through floor-to-ceiling windows. There's a fine dining restaurant, a rooftop pool and a chic spa.
D5 99 Union Street 206/749-7000 Central Link to University Street

HOTEL 1000

www.hotel1000seattle.com
Rooms at this service-first luxury hotel feature LCD HDTVs, high-speed wireless Internet, custom furnishings and lots more little extras.
D15 1000 1st Avenue 206/957-1000

HOTEL MONACO

www.monaco-seattle.com
Lively and stylish hotel with personable staff and a fun restaurant—Sazerac. Some of the 189 rooms have baths. Pet friendly.
E15 1101 4th Avenue 206/621-1770 or 800/715-6513

PAN PACIFIC SEATTLE

www.panpacific.com
In the heart of Downtown, this luxurious modern hotel couldn't be more convenient, and there are great city views from the upper floors. Rooms have huge windows, designer fittings and large bathtubs, and amenities include a spa and fitness center.
D12 2125 Terry Avenue 206/264-8111 or 877/324-4856

INN AT THE MARKET

This charming small hotel with French provincial decor shares a brick courtyard with the Café Campagne (▷ 42). Views over lovely Elliott Bay make this a stay to remember.
D14 86 Pine Street 206/443-3600 or 800/446-4484; www.innatthemarket.com

PARAMOUNT HOTEL

www.paramounthotelseattle.com
146 rooms and suites in the heart of Downtown. Newly built, the hotel leans toward classic English country lodges—dark wood furniture and a fireplace in the lobby.
E15 724 Pine Street 206/292-9500 8, 9, 60

SHERATON SEATTLE HOTEL & TOWERS

www.sheraton.com/seattle
Downtown tower with a striking lobby and 840 rooms filled with art by Northwest artists. Health club and restaurant.
E14 1400 6th Avenue 206/621-9000

SORRENTO HOTEL

www.hotelsorrento.com
Built in 1909, this landmark hotel's first guest was President William Taft. Now Seattle's most historic luxury hotel, its restaurant—the Hunt Club—is a local treasure.
F15 900 Madison Street 206/622-6400 12, 43, 49, 60

W SEATTLE

www.starwoodhotels.com
Modern and striking, this hotel is known for its W Signature Beds with down pillows and duvets. Plasma TVs, DVD and CD players in each room. The hotel's lounge is a great place to spot a celebrity.
E15 1112 4th Avenue 206/264-6000

Need to Know

The following section will help you plan your visit to Seattle. We have suggested the best ways to get around the city and provided useful information for while you are there.

Planning Ahead

When to Go

Seattle is a year-round destination and focal point for arts in the Pacific Northwest. Ringed by ski resorts, Seattle attracts winter sports enthusiasts, and sports fans visit during the baseball and football seasons. Hotel reservations are a must at any time of year.

TIME

Seattle is on Pacific Standard Time, three hours behind New York, eight hours behind the UK.

AVERAGE DAILY MAXIMUM TEMPERATURES

JAN	FEB	MAR	APR	MAY	JUN	JUL	AUG	SEP	OCT	NOV	DEC
45°F	50°F	53°F	59°F	66°F	70°F	76°F	75°F	69°F	62°F	51°F	47°F
7°C	10°C	12°C	13°C	19°C	21°C	24°C	24°C	20°C	16°C	10°C	8°C

Spring (March to May) brings a flurry of bulbs and flowering trees; weather can be unsettled.
Summer (June to August) is sunny and clear, with cool nights. Plan to dress in layers.
Fall (September to November) is often lovely, particularly September, with rainfall averaging 1.8in (5cm).
Winter (December to February) rarely brings snow to the city, although the Cascade and Olympic mountains receive vast quantities. November to January are the rainiest months.

WHAT'S ON

January/February *Chinese and Vietnamese New Year's Celebration.*
February/March *Fat Tuesday:* Mardi Gras celebration in Pioneer Square.
March *Moisture Festival.*
Seattle Boat Show.
April *Arcade Lights Artisan Food, Craft, Beer and Wine Festival* at Pike Place Market.
Cherry Blossom and Japanese Cultural Festival.
May *Opening Day of Yachting Season* (first Saturday).
Seattle Maritime Festival.
University District Street Fair.
Northwest Folklife Festival: The largest in the country.
Seattle International Film Festival.
June *Fremont Fair* (Jun 20–22): A celebration of the longest day.
Olympic Music Festival.
Seattle Pride.
July *4 July. Out to Lunch Summer:* Downtown concerts.
Lake Union Wooden Boat Festival.
Caribbean Festival–A Taste of Soul.
Chinatown International District Summer Festival.
Bite of Seattle Food Fest.
Seafair: Races on water featuring milk-carton derbies and hydrofoil heats plus tribal powwows and more.
September *Bumbershoot:* Festival of music, visual arts and crafts.
Chief Seattle Days: powwow.
Viking Days: weekend of reenactments, crafts and food in Ballard.
October–November *Earshot Jazz Festival.*
December *Christmas Ship:* Brightly lit vessels make the rounds of the beaches with caroling choirs aboard.

Seattle Online

www.visitseattle.org
The Seattle–King County Visitors Bureau website. Listings and a calendar of events.

www.seattle.citysearch.com/guide/seattle-wa-metro
Comprehensive city guide with travel, hotels, dining and entertainment listings, and a readers' rating system. Links to local weather information, with five-day forecasts and satellite photographs.

www.seattlemet.com/arts-and-entertainment
Pacific Northwest arts and entertainment guide, service of a local media company, with links to hotels, tours, transportation, shopping, restaurants and the outdoors.

www.tripplanner.kingcounty.gov
Helps you plan bus transportation from point A to B. Provides route numbers, stop locations, schedules and next-bus-out information.

www.wsdot.wa.gov/ferries
Official Washington State ferry website, with schedule and fare information.

www.graylineofseattle.com
Bus service between Sea-Tac airport and Downtown, plus bus tours. Also operates as Horizon Seattle.

www.seattle.hotelscheap.org/
Seattle area hotels reviewed and rated by guests. Includes last-minute deals and online reservations.

www.weather.com
Weather information by city and zip code; current conditions, 10-day forecast, weather alerts and satellite photographs.

www.Amtrak.com
Route, fare and schedule information and online booking for Amtrak rail service.

GOOD TRAVEL SITES

www.fodors.com
A complete travel-planning site. Research prices and weather; book air tickets, cars and rooms.

www.seattle.gov
A wide range of information for visitors includes the current week's events, large and small.

www.access.wa.gov
Everything you need to know to venture farther afield.

STAYING CONNECTED

Free WiFi is available all over the city. Starbucks and other coffee shops are prime spots, though you'll be expected to buy something. You can also get online at the Seattle Center, and in all of the city's public libraries. If you don't have a laptop or smartphone, the central library has computers for public use, available for 30 minutes with a guest pass or for longer if you buy a library card. Some businesses have open access too, and specific locations are listed on www.openwifispots.com, which enables you to search by neighborhood or category (bookstores, shopping malls, gas stations, etc).

Getting There

ENTRY REQUIREMENTS

International travelers going to the US under the Visa Waiver Program (VWP) are now subject to enhanced security requirements. Online completion and approval of ESTA (Electronic System for Travel Authorization), along with payment of the fee, is mandatory ahead of travel for all VWP travelers. For full details, go to the official website www.esta.cbp.dhs.gov.

CUSTOMS REGULATIONS

Duty-free allowances include 1 liter of alcoholic spirits or wine (no one under 21 may bring in alcohol), 200 cigarettes and 100 cigars (not Cuban) and up to $100-worth of gifts.
Some medications may be prescription-only in the US and may be confiscated. Bring a doctor's certificate for essential medication.

AIRPORT

Sea-Tac International Airport is 15 miles (24km) south of Downtown Seattle. Flights from New York take 5–6 hours, from LA 2–3 hours and from London about 10 hours. Upon arrival, look for the large airport maps near the escalators.

FROM SEA-TAC INTERNATIONAL AIRPORT
For airport information ☎ 206/787–5388 and there's an information desk near Baggage Claim. There are a variety of ways to get Downtown. Travel time is 30 minutes or more, depending on transportation mode and traffic conditions.

The Link Light Rail service runs Mon–Sat 5am–1am, Sun 6am–midnight, with trains every 7.5–15 minutes, depending on the time of day. It will get you to downtown Seattle in about 30 minutes and costs around $2.75.

The Downtown Airporter bus (☎ 855/566–3300) departs twice an hour (6.30am–9pm) from the inner drive curb on the 3rd floor of the Airport Garage, with service to and from major hotels; cost is about $18. King County Metro Transit buses leave from bus stops on International Boulevard (State Highway 99) and South 176th Street near the Link Light Rail Station; exact change is required and the ticket costs between $2.25 and $3 one-way (☎ 206/553–3000 or log on to the website, http://tripplanner.kingcounty.gov).

Taxis and limousines pick up passengers on the third floor of the parking garage, across

from the Main Terminal. Limousines also pick up at the curb outside Baggage Claim. Fares are around $43 to Downtown. Thirteen rental companies occupy the Rental Car Facility, reached by a 24-hour shuttle bus from outside Baggage Claim.

ARRIVING BY BUS

Greyhound (☎ 800/231–2222) buses arrive and leave from Seattle's Greyhound Terminal Downtown at 503 S Royal Brougham Way.

ARRIVING BY CAR

If you arrive by car you will enter the city via I–5. Downtown exits are Union Street (for City Center) and James Street (for Pioneer Square). If arriving via I–90 from the east you will cross the Homer M. Hadley Memorial Bridge; from there follow signs to I–5 north for Downtown exits. If you intend to rent a car and are not a US citizen, bring your foreign license and an international driver's license, which must be acquired before arriving. Most car rental agencies require a major credit card; many will not rent a car to persons under 25.

ARRIVING BY TRAIN

Amtrak trains (☎ 800/872–7245) arrive at King Street Station at 3rd and Jackson, between Pioneer Square and the International District. The journey from LA takes 29–35 hours. From New York, change trains in Chicago (NY–Chicago 18–21 hours, Chicago–Seattle 47 hours).

DRIVING IN SEATTLE

Slow-moving traffic and even gridlock is common on Interstate 5, Seattle's only North–South freeway. Avenues and streets may have either names or numbers, but virtually all have helpful directional designations (NE, SW). Downtown Seattle has both on-street metered parking and garages and lots. Most meters cost $2–$3 per hour, with a two-hour limit—and meter maids are vigilant. Unlimited free parking on Sunday.

VISITORS WITH DISABILITIES

Downtown Seattle streets, especially those running east to west, can be difficult for travelers with a disability because of the city's steep hills. Streets and public buildings are required to have ramps, and some neighborhoods are level and evenly paved. All of the city's buses have wheelchair lifts and designated space on the bus. For more information check the websites for Mobility International USA (www.miusa.org) and Access-Able Travel Source (www.access-able.com) ☎ 303/232–2979.

Getting Around

ETIQUETTE

- Seattle dress is informal; for most places, a jacket and tie are optional.
- Seattle has a successful recycling program. Many public places provide recycling bins. Littering is not tolerated.
- Smoking is prohibited in public places.
- Tipping 15–20 percent is customary in restaurants; 15 percent for taxis.

SAFETY

- Exercise caution and at night avoid the areas around 1st to 2nd and Pike, the edges of Pioneer Square, Northgate between 3rd and 5th, and most of all the area between 2nd and 4th from James to Yesler.
- Seattle police are well known for giving out tickets to jaywalkers.

METRO BUSES

- For Metro Rider Information ☎ 206/553–3000 or 206/296-0100; also online information at www.metro.gov.
- Seventeen bus routes use the Downtown Seattle Transit Tunnel under Pine Street and 3rd Avenue, with five downtown stations: Convention Place, Westlake, University Street, Pioneer Square and the International District. Sunday and evenings after hours, when the tunnel is closed, tunnel buses run above ground (the website gives route information).
- More than 200 other bus routes serve the city and outlying areas. Fares range from $2.25–$3 and cash must be put into the farebox next to the driver. You can also purchase a rechargeable ORCA card ($5), valid on buses, trains and ferries in the Puget Sound area. For information, visit www.orcacard.com/ERG-Seattle.
- Seattle bus drivers are not required to call out the stops along the route. Ask your driver to alert you once you have reached your stop.

LINK LIGHT RAIL

- The Central Link line runs for more than 14 miles (23km) between downtown Seattle and Sea-Tac International Airport, and has 13 stations
- Trains run every 7.5–10 minutes, and fares are $2–$2.75 one way.
- A 3.5-mile (5.6km) underground extension is set to reach the University of Washington in 2016 then press onward to Northgate by 2021.
- For information, schedules and a trip planner, visit www.soundtransit.org.

MONORAIL

- The Monorail between Downtown Westlake Center and Seattle Center takes only 90 seconds. Trains run every 10–15 minutes; weekdays 7.30am–11pm and weekends 8.30am–11pm.
- Adult tickets cost $2.25 per ride and can be purchased on the third floor of Westlake Center and at Seattle Center beneath the Space Needle.
- For details, visit www.seattlemonorail.com.

SEATTLE STREETCAR

- Although the vintage Waterfront Streetcar has gone, a modern streetcar now runs from Pioneer Square up to South Lake Union, with 11 stops, and there are plans to expand the system.
- Streetcars run every 10–15 minutes, Mon–Thu 6am–9pm, Fri–Sat 6am–11pm, Sun and holidays 10–7. The one-way fare is $2.50 and ORCA cards are accepted.
- For information ☎ 206/553–3000 or visit www.seattlestreetcar.org.

TAXIS

- Taxis are expensive—get one at your hotel or call for a radio-dispatched cab. Many Seattle taxis are not authorized to pick up passengers hailing them from the street, so it's best to call ahead. Two of the largest and most reputable companies are Yellow Cab (☎ 206/622–6500) and Orange Cab (☎ 206/522–8800).
- Cab services can become incredibly busy on Friday and Saturday evenings. Call up to one hour in advance.
- The flag-drop charge is $2.50 and it's $2.70 for each additional mile. Depending on the price of gas at the time, a fuel surcharge may be imposed.

WASHINGTON STATE FERRIES

- Jumbo ferries from Seattle's Downtown terminal to Bainbridge Island and Bremerton (on the Kitsap Peninsula) depart regularly from Colman Dock at pier 52. They take walk-on passengers and cars.
- Most ferry routes are busy during weekday commute periods and on sunny weekends. Expect waits of two hours or more in summer.
- Schedules change seasonally: ☎ 206/464–6400 or visit www.wsdot.wa.gov/ferries for information.
- Additional ferry routes departing from the Seattle environs serve the Kitsap Peninsula, Vashon Island, Whidbey Island, Port Townsend (Olympic Peninsula), the San Juan Islands and Victoria, British Columbia (Canada).

DISCOUNTS

- Ticket/Ticket: Half-price day-of-show tickets (cash only)—theater, concert, dance, comedy and music available at two locations: Pike Place Market Info Booth ✉ 1st Avenue and Pike Street and Broadway Market, 401 Broadway E on Capitol Hill ☎ 206/461–5840 ⏲ Closed Mon
- A CityPass ticket book will reduce admission prices by 47 percent to Woodland Park Zoo or Experience Music Project, Space Needle, Pacific Science Center or Museum of Flight, Seattle Aquarium and Argosy Cruises Harbor Tour. Passbooks are valid for nine days.
- Student travelers are advised to bring a current student ID to obtain discounted admissions.

ORGANIZED TOURS

- Gray Line Tours/Horizon Seattle: a variety of ways to see Seattle (☎ 206/626–5200 or 800/426–7532; www.graylineofseattle.com)
- Seattle Seaplanes: get a bird's-eye view of the city (☎ 206/329–9638; www.seattleseaplanes.com)
- Argosy Tours: take a harbor or lake cruise (206/623–1445; www.argosycruises.com)
- BeelineTours: explore by bus (206/632–5162; www.beelinetours.com)

Essential Facts

MONEY

- Money-changing facilities are available at Sea-Tac Airport, banks and at Travelex Currency Service on level 3 of Westlake Center in Downtown Seattle ☎ 206/682–4525.
- Most major establishments and businesses accept major credit cards. Few places accept personal checks; bring traveler's checks.
- Automatic Teller Machines (ATMs) are available at most banks.

CURRENCY

The unit of currency is the dollar (= 100 cents). Bills (notes) come in denominations of $1, $5, $10, $20, $50 and $100; coins are 25¢ (a quarter), 10¢ (a dime), 5¢ (a nickel) and 1¢ (a penny).

24-HOUR PHARMACIES

- Bartell Drug Store ✉ 600 1st Avenue N (near Seattle Center) ☎ 206/284–1354 and several other locations.
- Walgreen Drug Store ✉ 5409 15th Avenue NW ☎ 206/781–0056 and several other locations.

ELECTRICITY

- 110 volts, 60 cycles AC current.
- Electrical outlets are for flat, two-prong plugs. European appliances require an adaptor and a converter.

LAVATORIES

Public lavatories are located in Pike Place Market and in the Convention Center.

LOST PROPERTY

- Airport lost and found ☎ 206/787–5312
- King Street Station lost and found ☎ 206/382–4713
- Metro bus lost and found ☎ 206/553–3000 and press 0.

MAIL

The main Downtown post office is on the corner of Union and 3rd Avenue
🕒 Mon–Fri 8.30–5.30; closed Sat–Sun.
☎ 800/275–8777 for 24-hour infoline with zip codes, postal rates, post office hours and location; or www.usps.com. Stamps are sold at many supermarket check-outs.

NATIONAL HOLIDAYS

New Year's Day (Jan 1); Martin Luther King Day (3rd Mon in Jan); President's Day (3rd Mon in Feb); Memorial Day (last Mon in May); Independence Day (Jul 4); Labor Day (1st Mon in Sep); Columbus Day (2nd Mon in Oct); Veterans' Day (Nov 11); Thanksgiving (4th Thu in Nov); Christmas Day (Dec 25)

NEWSPAPERS AND MAGAZINES

- Seattle has two daily papers: *The Seattle*

Times ☎ 206/464–2111 and the *Seattle Post-Intelligencer* ☎ 206/448–8030.
- Free weeklies that provide entertainment listings include the alternative *Stranger* and *The Weekly*.
- The *Seattle Gay News* is a community newspaper ☎ 206/324–4297.
- International newspapers are sold at First and Pike News (✉ 93 Pike Street at the Pike Place Market) and at Bulldog News (✉ 4208 University Way NE).

OPERATING HOURS
- Banks: Generally Mon–Fri 9.30–5, some open Saturday mornings.
- Offices: Normally Mon–Fri 9–5.
- Stores in Downtown open 9–10am and typically close at 5–6pm, with some staying open until 9pm on Thursday evenings. Shops in shopping malls generally stay open Mon–Sat until 9pm; Sun until 5 or 6pm.

PLACES OF WORSHIP
Check the Yellow Pages of the phone book for complete listings. Some of the prominent houses of worship are listed below:
- Catholic: St. James Cathedral ✉ 9th Avenue and Marion Street ☎ 206/622–3559
- Congregational: Plymouth Congregational Church ✉ 6th Avenue and University Street ☎ 206/622–4865
- Episcopal: St. Mark's Episcopal Cathedral ✉ 1245 10th Avenue E ☎ 206/323–0300
- Greek Orthodox: St. Demetrios Greek Orthodox Church ✉ 2100 Boyer Avenue E ☎ 206/631–2500
- Lutheran: Gethsemane Lutheran Church ✉ 9th Avenue and Stewart Street ☎ 206/682–3620
- Methodist: First United Methodist ✉ 811 5th Avenue ☎ 206/622–7278
- Mosque: Islamic (Idris) Mosque ✉ 1420 NE Northgate Way ☎ 206/363–3013
- Synagogue: Temple De Hirsch Sinai ✉ 1511 E Pike Street ☎ 206/323–8486

CONSULATES
- British ✉ 900 4th Avenue, Suite 3001 ☎ 206/622–9255
- Canadian ✉ 412 Plaza 600, 6th Avenue and Stewart Street ☎ 206/443–1777
- French ✉ 2200 Alaskan Way, Suite 490 ☎ 206/256–6184
- Japanese ✉ 601 Union Street, Suite 500 ☎ 206/682–9107

VISITOR INFORMATION
- Seattle Visitor Center and Concierge Services ✉ Upper Pike Street Lobby in the Convention Center (7th and Pike) ☎ 206/461–5840; www.visitseattle.org 🕒 Mon–Fri 9–5 year-round; also Sat–Sun 10–5 Memorial Day–Labor Day
- Seattle Center Info ☎ 206/684–7200
- Seattle Public Library offers a Quick Information number ☎ 206/386–4636; www.spl.org

EMERGENCY PHONE NUMBERS

- Police, ambulance or fire 911
- The Red Cross Language Bank provides free, on-call interpretive assistance in emergency or crisis situations. Volunteers in more than 60 languages 206/323–2345

MEDICAL TREATMENT

- It is vital to have comprehensive insurance.
- US HealthWorks operates several drop-in clinics; nearest clinic to Downtown is the clinic at Denny and Fairview 206/682–7418 Mon–Fri 7am–6pm, Sat 9–5. Also at 836 NE Northgate Way 206/784–0737 Mon–Fri 8am–7pm, Sat 10am–4pm and 3223 1st Avenue S, Suite C 206/624–3651 Mon–Fri 6am–4.30pm
- Dentist Referral Service 206/443–7607; www.skcds.org

WEIGHTS & MEASURES

Metric equivalents for US weights and measures:

- Weights:
1 ounce (oz) = 28 grams;
1 pound (lb) = 0.45 kilogram;
1 quart (qt) = 0.9 liter (L).
- Measurements:
1 inch (") = 2.5 centimeters;
1 foot (') = 0.3 meter;
1 yard (yd) = 0.9 meter;
1 mile = 1.6 kilometers

TELEPHONES

To call Seattle from the UK dial 00 1 (the code for the US), followed by the area code, then the 7-digit number. To call the UK from Seattle, dial 011 44 then drop the first zero from the area code. To make a local call from a pay phone, listen for a dial tone, then deposit coins; wait for new dial tone and dial the number.

Phonecards for long-distance calls are available at most shops and some phones take credit cards. To pay cash for long-distance calls, follow the same initial procedure as for local calls, and a recorded operator message will tell you how much additional money to deposit for the first three minutes; then deposit additional coins and dial.

The area code for Seattle is 206. The area running east of Lake Washington from Everett to Maple Valley and east to Snoqualmie pass uses area code 425. The 253 area code runs south from Renton to the Pierce-Thurston county line. Other calls within western Washington require dialing a 360 area code. Directory assistance is a toll call. For information, dial 411 or 1 plus the area code, plus 555–1212.

Using your cell (mobile) phone abroad can incur hefty roaming charges. Consider having your phone unlocked by your service provider and installing a new SIM card suited to your destination, or pick up an inexpensive pay-as-you-go phone after you arrive. You can also turn off your data roaming, then find a WiFi hot spot and use a service such as Skype, Google Talk or iChat.

TELEVISION AND RADIO

- Seattle's two National Public Radio stations (NPR) are KUOW at 94.9 FM (all-talk radio with news from the BBC) and KPLU, an award-winning jazz station at 88.5 FM.
- KING-FM (98.1) Classical music.
- Seattle's local TV channels are: KOMO 4 (ABC); KING 5 (NBC); KIRO 7 (CBS); KCTS/9 (PBS); KZJO 22 (MNT); KFFV 45 (independent).

Culinary Tours

Foodies are flocking to Seattle to savor the upsurge in fine dining, led by some of the nation's most accomplished chefs and innovative restaurateurs. The gourmet pubs, chic bistros and restaurants also benefit from the region's dedicated farmers, fishers and artisan food producers. What to wash it all down with? Investigate the burgeoning beer culture, craft distilleries and wineries. Tracking down the best of the best on a short visit can be tricky, but tour companies devote their entire business to this—here are a few to whet your appetite.

BON VIVANT WINE TOURS

www.bonvivanttours.com

In addition to the Woodinville wineries, this company sometimes heads out to places like Bainbridge Island, Yakima or Leavenworth.

☎ 206/524-8687 Duration usually 6–7 hours, sometimes longer $89–$135

LOCAL CRAFT DISTILLERY TOURS

www.localcrafttours.com

Three craft distilleries are toured, and you'll meet the master distillers, hear about the history of distilling and prohibition, learn the secret to a good cocktail and sample plenty of spirits and a couple of cocktails.

☎ 206/455-3740 Duration $89, includes a take-home gift

ROAD DOG BREWERY TOURS

www.roaddogtours.com

This company will be your designated driver on a tour that includes three craft breweries or micro-distilleries. Coffee tours visit several selected coffee shops, with a bakery thrown in.

☎ 206/249-9858 Duration 3 hours $79, non-drinkers $20

SAVOR SEATTLE FOOD TOURS

www.savorseattletours.com

Six themed walking tours within Seattle range from a guided stroll around Pike Place Market, with tastings and behind-the-scenes visits, to eating your way around five of the city's finest restaurants (yes, on one tour).

☎ 206/209-5485 Times vary. Duration 2 hours $39.99–$69.99

SEATTLE BITES FOOD TOURS

www.seattlebitesfoodtours.com

Meet the merchants at Pike Place Market and taste generous portions of food prepared specially for you. You'll also learn about the history of the market.

☎ 425/888-8837 Daily at 10.30; also at 2.30 May–Sep. Duration 2.5 hours $39.99

SEATTLE FOOD TOURS

www.seattlefoodtours.com

Tour Belltown or Capitol Hill on a progressive dinner tour of five restaurants. They also offer a tour of Pike Place Market with a chef, picking up ingredients for a cookery demonstration.

☎ 206/725-4483 Duration 2.5–3 hours $39.99–$99

SEATTLE WINE TOURS

www.seattlewinetours.com

The Woodinville area has more than 100 wineries, and you'll visit some on these luxury customized tours.

☎ 206/444-9463 Duration 4 hours to multi-day tours From $299 for up to four people

WHITE MOUSTACHE ADVENTURE COMPANY

www.whitemoustache.com

Private tours are customized to your needs, and there's no walking. A minimum of four stops are made, and tasting themes include a progressive breakfast, seafood and beer.

☎ 206/552-0950 Duration 3–4 hours $250 for two people, $100 per extra adult

Timeline

CHIEF SEALTH

Sealth was born in 1786 on Blake Island. In 1792, the young boy watched "the great canoe with giant white wings"—Captain Vancouver's brig—sail into Puget Sound. In his twenties he became leader of the Suquamish, Duwamish and allied bands, and became a friend to white settlers. One, the pioneer Arthur Denny, suggested changing the settlement's name from Alki to Sealth, which, being difficult for whites to pronounce, was soon corrupted to Seattle. Preceding the Indian War of 1856, Governor Isaac Stevens drafted a settlement promising the native tribes payments and reservation lands. Fearing his people's ways would disappear in the face of the growing number of settlers, Sealth reluctantly signed.

1792 British Captain George Vancouver and his lieutenant, Peter Puget, explore the "inland sea," which Vancouver names Puget Sound.

1851 David Denny, John Low and Lee Terry reach Alki Point and dub their colony "New York–Alki."

1852 Pioneers move the settlement across Elliott Bay to what is now Pioneer Square.

1853 Henry Yesler begins operating a steam sawmill, establishing the timber industry. President Fillmore signs an act creating the Washington Territory. (Washington achieves statehood in 1889.)

1856 The so-called "Indian War": US battle sloop *Decatur* fires into Downtown to root out native peoples, who burn the settlement.

1869 The city is incorporated and passes its first public ordinance—a law against drunkenness.

1889 The Great Seattle Fire causes damage exceeding $10 million.

1893 James Hill's Great Northern Railroad reaches its western terminus, Seattle.

1897 The ship *Portland* steams into Seattle carrying "a ton of gold" and triggers the Klondike Gold Rush.

Totem poles in Pioneer Square and a memorial to Chief Sealth recall a time when the area was a Suquamish settlement (left, right); a statue of Lenin, Fremont (middle)

1909 The construction of Lake Washington Ship Canal begins, ending in 1917.

1919 The Seattle General Strike—60,000 workers walk off the job.

1940 The Lake Washington Floating Bridge, now the Lacey V. Murrow Memorial Bridge, links Seattle with Eastside communities.

1941 The US enters World War II. Workers flood Seattle to work in the shipyards and elsewhere.

1949 An earthquake measuring 7.2 on the Richter scale strikes the area.

1980 Mount St. Helens erupts, showering ash over Seattle, 100 miles (161km) away.

1999 The World Trade Organization meets in Seattle. Protesters take to the streets.

2001 An earthquake measuring 6.8 on the Richter scale rocks Seattle, causing more than $1billion in damage.

2005 Seattle wins the distinction of Most Literate City in the United States.

2012 Launch of the Waterfront Seattle plan to enhance the Central Waterfront area for public use, improve access and replace the decaying Elliott Bay Seawall. Seattle Great Wheel opens.

CORPORATE HISTORY

- 1970: Boeing's decision to lay off 655,000 workers over a two-year period precipitates a recession.
- 1971: Starbucks opens in Pike Place Market, launching the nation's specialty coffee craze.
- 1975: Bill Gates and Paul Allen start Microsoft.
- 2000: The US Justice Department anti-trust rulings order the breakup of Microsoft. Microsoft appeals.
- 2001: Boeing moves its HQ to Chicago. The Seattle area reels from the dot.com collapse.
- 2013: Boeing records more than $86 billion in sales; its huge manufacturing complex remains the city's largest employer.
- 2014: City announces the phasing in of a minimum wage of $15 per hour, the highest in the US.

Native American art (left, right); the bronze statue of a halibut fisherman that tops the Fishermen's Memorial in the terminal; the base is inscribed with names of fishermen who have lost their lives at sea (middle)

Index

TITLES IN THE SERIES

- Amsterdam
- Barcelona
- Boston
- Budapest
- Chicago
- Dubai
- Dublin
- Edinburgh
- Florence
- Hong Kong
- Istanbul
- Las Vegas
- Lisbon
- London
- Madrid
- Milan
- Montréal
- Munich
- New York City
- Orlando
- Paris
- Rome
- San Francisco
- Seattle
- Shanghai
- Singapore
- Sydney
- Tokyo
- Toronto
- Venice
- Washington, D.C.